High In The Mountains Somewhere Over China, A Bird Reels and Floats

High In The Mountains Somewhere Over China, A Bird Reels and Floats

By

One Who Waits

Copyright © 2009 by Gary Jones

All rights reserved. No part of this book may be reproduced, stored, or transmitted by any means—whether auditory, graphic, mechanical, or electronic—without written permission of both publisher and author, except in the case of brief excerpts used in critical articles and reviews. Unauthorized reproduction of any part of this work is illegal and is punishable by law.

ISBN: 978-0-578-01395-4

Dedication

In loving memory of Bodi,
Or Bodidharma Moon, his full given name,
Who never left my side.
He was truly this man's best friend,
Until I took his collar and lead off one day
      somewhere near Bainbridge Island,
And never saw him again.
Wherever you are now my true companion,
I hope things are going well, and you get
      laid often.
Or, at least, occasionally.
I will always remember to never forget,
      sleeping in the snow under the starry
      night with you on the Quinault
      River.
Go in peace my friend.

Other Titles I Considered For This Edition

[Offered here for the entertainment of the reader and for possible use in my next book, if it ever comes]

I Came From Outer Space

Once Upon a Time in Nowhere

Man From the Stars
[How One Alien Crash Landed On Earth and Put An End to Violence and Stupidity Forever]

The Lighthouse Keeper

Starman

Sleepwalker

Bodidharma Moon

Bodidharma and The Dog Girl From the Moon

Brother Wind, Sister Moon

Bodidharma and the Poppy Field

I, Poet

One Who Waits

The Opium Smoker

Star Light, Star Bright, First Star I See Tonight

I Am No One

Dream, Dream, Dream...

Beautiful Dreamer

The Children's Crusade

The Anarchaic Poet

Archaea and the Evolutionary Reversal of Consciousness

Greybeard

Contents

Author's Preface xiii
Opening 1
Where am I now? 4
I Think, I Wait, I Fast 7
From a Star Beyond the Dark Carnivale 10
The High Mountain Range 11
Unbecoming 13
Here You Are Now, My Poets 16
The Clowns Slowly Fade 19
The Ruling Class 21
For The Landlords 24
The Belly Of The Beast 26
My Brother, My Sister 28
The Time Is Now 31
Shoulder Your Duds Dear One 33
Coming This Way I Caution You... 35
Will You Meet Me There? 36
A Short Walk 37
Mon Sheri 48
Romantic Western Love 54

Looni Bird 56

My Sweet Cold Ocean 62

Breathing 63

The Rain Forest 64

After Midnight 66

the color blue 67

two women..68

before dawn 86

waking 87

Dreaming 88

Twilight 89

Lynette 90

Message for Lynette...92

Sand..93

Ghost Riders...96

Mon Sheri, how did we miss each other?........................98

For Lynette...101

The Mercer Island Tunnel and The House on Phinney Ridge..102

The Virgin Meets Albert Hoffmann 104

The Matsen Farms...108

Brother Wolf...117

Brenda, Sister Moon 120

Taeya 122

Summer Solstice	124
Songs From Deep Regions	127
Meeting Old Friends	129
One Drop	130
Mary	131
Night Watch	132
Wands	133
Patty Jo	134
Bright Eyes	135
In A Garden Bright	136
Song of November	137
Water	138
When I Die	139
Mary in Rainbows	140
Is The Unwrapping Done	141
O' Stranger	142
Letters To My Friend	143
My dearest darling	145
Who Am I Today?	147
North to Alaska, or the Story of Balto:	149
Evgeniya, Ethereal Soviet	150
Note to ….	151
6/12/08	153
6/13/08	154

7/14/08	155
6/18/08	156
6/18/08	157
Cantina Mia	159
Song for All Seasons	162

Author's Preface

Since somewhere near the beginning of time as I know it, people have been encouraging me to write a book. You know, just write a book. Alright everyone; here it is. Here is Gary's book. I even changed my name to One Who Waits, an approximate Athabasca tribalization of who I think I am, since I have no real affinity to my "given" name. I made up this compound word, as you may have noticed. This is something I do often, as language, like human consciousness, is vaguely evolutionary in its progress. Although I have always felt that evolution makes more sense when you argue from the most complex to the least. And it only makes sense within the questionable context of linear time, and who lives there? Bacteria and viruses will likely inherit the earth, in my thinking, along with a lot of insects. What is time again? This book is also for my true companion, because I love her. I may still have the little red book she bought for me when I was a boy. It was full of blank, white pages, nice, high quality cottony stuff. It actually felt good to touch these empty pages with my fingers. The idea was for me to fill it with words and ideas, and then give it back to her, I think. So it goes...And if you are still out there, my most beautiful, darling young one, here is your book, bright eyes. Call me some time. I would love to ravage your body. Or just get drunk with you. And then ravage your body...Or we could discuss the book. And then I could...you know. The fact is, my true companion is out there. She does not respond to my letters or messages. As of last summer, she also has no name. So it goes...

My father's maiden name was Jones, some Welsh derivative I hear. This name appears on most legal documents and licenses I own. But my father was an asshole, and we no longer celebrate his birthday. We party on his deadday. The day he died. The most profound contribution Don Jones made to this planet was by dying and removing his influence on others forever. The exact date of his departure from the big blue marble was sometime during the fall of the Gregorian calendar, in the year 2000. No one cares exactly, except perhaps the state, in their infinite wisdom. Settle the accounts you know. After the big war, he worked for some 30 years, off and on, as a banker and briefly as a counselor at the women's prison in Purdy, Washington. He was a money lender, you know? My inheritance was an empty leather wallet and coin purse. I do keep these, as they are perfectly symbolic of everything Don was; beautiful on the outside, well oiled, full of nothing, and some small change. Oh, and some mineralized carbon remnants in a little oriental urn. I poured these into the mortared window sill of the Harvester restaurant and lounge in the Stadium District of Tacoma, Washington. After watering them in with the remaining contents of a vodka martini, he blended in quite nicely. Next time you are at the Harvester, find the corner window seat to the southeast more or less, and slam a couple in honor of "Old Bones."

I was raised by my mom, Louise, and my sister Cheryl. My mother's maiden name is far more colorful: Doubleday. We have no connection to the publishing house, unfortunately. Although I am told Abner Doubleday is a distant relative and the first real American President of the Theosophist Society, a pseudo-mystical philosophical group formed around the dawn of the United States, a country formed of rebels and miscreants from greater and lesser Europe. You know, America the Beautiful. A nation state, really, stolen from native tribes that were thousands of years their precedents through butchery, deception, and the law of mass numbers. Abner was also a general in the civil war, and while still a major with the northern forces, gave the command to fire on southern troops at Fort Sumter, thus heralding the beginning of the war proper. The shot heard round the world? One of the most horrific bloodbaths in history. Something nice for your resume? My sister loved to read to me, when I was a sprightly little boy. She adored me, for some reason. I remember clearly sitting at the top of the stairs in summer, hefting a gigantic encyclopedia around, with its slippery pages and lots of images of things from around the great wide world. After my father abandoned the family when my sister contracted diabetes, and not too long after I was born, these two wonderful women raised me, and encouraged me to write. Write a book, you know. My mom always worked, and married again when I was around 10 years old. His name is Bob Wilson, a divorced, starving teacher and musician she met while cruising the bars in Tacoma. We lived more or less in rational bliss, and I credit these people mostly for the fact that I am not completely fucked up, like almost everyone else I meet on this planet. Thanks you guys. You are my tribe, and I am already missing you...

So here is my book. Like all good poets, I have attempted to turn my self inside out, so to speak. To take what most people see as reflections of the light that occurs without, and reveal it from it's source, the light that occurs or is reflected from within...the third eye.

And all this for your benefit and amusement. It is a loosely organized collection of what I like to call word pictures, or painting with language. Straight from Nino the Mind Boggler to you..."look down my son, the snake is a river." And they soared on each others thoughts until the next morning and on into the next day when they were met by an ancient cockroach in a sombrero known only as "Don Brouhaha."

One Who Waits

Opening

You there, who pause so leisurely along the street this day,
With so casual an attitude about you.
Why do you linger, and what do you see?
Am I now invisible to you and to your kind?
Is this place so foreign I must reform my physical existence each time I visit?
Am I one who has no name, no concept in your earthly tongues?
Am I utterly unknown to you?

This I do know, and this I am happy to share with you, whoever you are.
I am old...older than time as you know it.
I am borne of the stars, and return to the stars for there is my home, my eternal space and dwelling.
Short and illusory are the moments I spend with you.
Your ways are strange to me, as you are strange.
And as we turn our separate ways, this you knew, while looking vacantly into my eyes.
In this instant, we exchange light, and are of the same conscious mind.
I know you, and you know me as well.
Most humans turn quickly away...they are terrified to think this knowledge makes them immediately transparent.
A million suns turn fire to ice and the frost consumes me.
The gifts I bring are free, however.
I ask nothing in return.

I will show you ways to avoid your great stupidity.
As of yet, you do not realize how necessary this is.
Or that the ways are simple.
This I can and will do for you.
You may not know that I was here, that these things I
    do are for you.
I do this because I love you.
I am the mystery that to this very moment,
Of this very day, eludes you.
You are lost, dear friends, and I am here to show your
    pony the way back home.

I open my eyes, and your world forms around me.
It is like I am waking from a dream, but the dream
    continues on...
As if a longer journey is ending momentarily, a
    waypoint,
And I must gather my things and take leave of the great
    ship that transported me.
And before my field of vision, or my conscious eye,
New vistas reveal themselves, new worlds, old worlds,
    worlds within worlds.
Sometimes what I become is familiar, sometimes it is
    strange.
But always, there is a sense of great effort and loss,
And my desire is to close my eyes again, to become light,
    energy, dreams, and go where I cannot take you,
    where I can hardly begin to describe to you...

I become aware of this body that propels me.
It contains what is my essential nature, an energetic
    form beyond your knowledge,
Beyond the forms and ideas that are familiar to you,
You are the earth beings, fixed dwellers, what you think
    is knowledge is the spring rose.

You are emergent in your collectiveness, like toddling
    children in a schoolyard.
Your race is volatile as are you and your kindred,
As are the smaller beastlings you spawn and nourish.
Are they not ever so precious?
I see your little boy push your little girl, I see the little
    girl strike the little boy,
I see the blood, hear the screaming, as the pain
    shimmers through me and is discarded.
You must be cautiously managed, often caged or
    destroyed.
You brutalize those who would love and befriend you,
    and feed upon them, like a viral contamination.

Where am I now?

This ever repeating process of becoming, then unbecoming, and becoming again.
Endlessly repeating like a slowly turning solar system or far galaxy...
There is a sound of water, and the sky looms far above,
This I see, blue and white, and soft, soothing cloud vapors.
A cooling wind blooms occasionally to caress me from the radiant heat of your sun.
My eyes roll downward, over the length of my body, and there is a dark blue sea. Separated by sand and gravel, and skittering crabs and insects, the sea floats and throbs.
It hums continuously, conspiring to roll over and take me, and all that I am, into itself.

We shudder together in sexual ecstasy, as I float in human form, and the sea devours me.
We are the same, the ocean and I, who am her brother, and she my terrible sister.
Her power diminishes all who confront her.
Diminishes all but me.
We are companions, and we adore the smell and touch of ourselves.
And the sky above goes forever on and we are carried away in the vastness of it...

So much effort, to acquire this body, this weight,
The ten thousand orchestrations that must occur to make it operate.

One Who Waits

How you bear this day after unending day I will never understand.
No, not today, not now, not for this only…they are children, how can they know.
It does not matter…the beautiful sighing breath of a bird, she does not matter.
In the twilight I vanish, and am gone…
Somewhere over China, a star falls from the sky, shimmering icicle rain.

Cold, cold water, I feel it on my toes.
I feel the red crab tugging on my finger, testing me for consumption,
Deciding finally against it.
The crab is wise, and knows in it's ancient soul which one of us is the true prey.
Every carbon atom, every false step of it's ancestors, have taught it this.
It knows, without knowing why.
I watch as he glides under the waters foamy edge.
How easily he makes the transition from one world to another.
He must know the water world is where he belongs, as he becomes buoyant and floated,
Washed in the sensuous atmosphere of salt and brine.
I think he is smiling as his now yellowish form shimmers in the water,
I assume this light, in the ocean that is me.
It disperses again, far and wide and deep, flowing on to the swirling galaxies, dripping in the grass and the rainbow colored flowers that bobble in the spring breeze.
I place one into my mouth and chew the bitter drug it contains.

Water to water...photon to photon, we are not so far different, we are not so far away from each other...this is the realm of the crab and the human being and the little flower.

I am back.
And I too am the little red crab.
I am on this ocean beach, floating in the sun, on the sand,
The red crab sees me diminish on the glimmering sand as the sloping shore break carries him slowly down hill toward the deepening ocean.
I recede in the distance as shimmering starlight.

I Think, I Wait, I Fast

So much effort to rise, to become again, to open these eyes and see.
Where is the red crab?
Gone through the looking glass, I imagine.
Down with the squirts and the oysters.
I roll my head to the side and see the dune grasses moving like hula dancers on the sand.
The entire scene is bathed in a curious lavender hue, like mist at the base of some distant waterfall.
Down in the narrow gullies between the dunes rise pale cinnamon colored mushrooms.
Dark blue are the stems with thick, rubbery caps.
I reach over cautiously and place the largest fattest one in my mouth, chewing deliberately, and finally swallowing.
Through the eons I have come to consume my self in this manner.
The spores of my blood, silent and invisible, float in the solar, galactic winds,
And propagate in the star bodies themselves, in the woods and fields of their planets.
We have long been upon the earth, so verdant, moist and green.

Fantasia streams before the dimensional theater of my inner eye.
Wild eyed creatures, animal caricatures mostly, dance in continuing streams,
Across a medieval landscape, tiny birds cling to the rocks and move up the roaring waterfalls...

Elaborate castles appear in the clouds, floating majestically, reorganizing as I watch.
A tiny mouse in a sorcerer's suit bobbles down a spiral stairway, grinning at me.
A clown in a monkey suit, kisses the theological beast.
Women and babies burn,
Skins fired to crisp chocolate and black down in the valley.
The emperor comes riding on his great horse with perfect white teeth.
While the senates debate,
Blue eyed babies lie dying in the rain,
So many millions of little blood puddings in the landscape.
They melt and are consumed by time and maggots...
The little dead ones nod in agreement,
All is for the better, for the advancement of the races.
Here is the fire of the world.
Here the overwhelming stench of your kind.
I cannot help my self...I vomit, then vomit again, until there is nothing more left to regurgitate.
Here are the final glories of your politicians and government administrators,
These priests have trained you to think of them benevolently as, The State.
[These same will track and pursue me, I assure you, for what I have written here today, in these poems, these songs of the greybeard. My love for you and the children of your house, ensure my doom, and the pursuit of my kind. They are watching me now, as I conspire to come to your immediate aid]
Praise the gentry classes who cajole you into a sleepy stupor.
Who numb your minds with insipid trivia and petty endeavors.
Shine your shoes and press your finest white linens,

Go forth in business and prosper.
Trophies glitter in the window, in the shattered glass of Las Vegas afternoons,
Who is the shepherd now, closing the gate quietly on the sleeping herd at evening light?
The dogs snuffle around my feet, awakening in their primordial minds, for this is their time, settled in the perimeter, protecting this pack, and with great stealth, cunning, and abandonment of self.

Riding forth, the trumpeting glory of the human being.
Here is the horned song of civilization, here is your bloodied stanchion.
I gaze upon the mighty warriors, and I weep over their dead bodies.
Bodies piled by the millions over the fields and valleys of this green earth,
A revolving planet hurtles forward through space, mindless in it's orbit.
Repeating for an eternity of eternities.

From a Star Beyond the Dark Carnivale

You ride a grain of sand on the tides of tomorrows senate,
Let us bring this to committee, to banal unending drivel.
Wildly grinning your blathering clowns of horror gather in the market.
You are the ruling class, the gentry of madness and consumption.

I saw a man today, whose eyes were blown out by a handgun in his hired taxi..
Fleshy pockets, dried grapes, sunken eye sockets where light once flowed.
He was smiling and laughing with the camera crew.
The shooter got away with a five dollar fare.
I talked to the cop who worked it.
It was a twenty-two caliber squirrel gun...
High in the mountains somewhere over China, a bird reels and floats.

The High Mountain Range

Oh pitiful unborn, reach and caress the fire that consumes you.
In an instant it devours us.
You become a gelatinous blob of moist tissue.
This is your civilization advancing on earth.
This your forbearers have wrought for thee.
Your mothers and fathers bring forth the past, in it's form eternal, and I am sick.
I am no part of it.

Take me!
Take this instead!
What ever I was and whatever I am or may become!
I will die in your place. Take all I have in fortune and wealth.
This I will gladly do for you and yours, and for all to come for the next 10,000 eternities.

Take it from me, and go.
Go to your cold mountain, with your gold and mythical dragons.
Leave me my coat and some good boots, that I may travel away from you.
That I may walk alone in the forest, in the rain with the silent eternal trees,
Croaking in the winds, the eternal winds of Asia.
Far and away, where the water is huge, and the signs of humans dwindle,
Where the smell of your civilization loses it's stink.

Where the hate and murder of your governments may
 not reach.
Let me go and become unstupid.
Coddling their masses in the comfort of churches and
 governances.
False ideologies and doctrines that convince and deceive.
We are wonderful, we are the civilized and enlightened
 ones.
And still the children burn in their skins,
Beautiful young soldiers and the natural landscapes of
 nations and what are not nations.
For thousands of ages, you continue.
You rise one on each, to methodically replace those who
 go before,
You change form, you move over the lands and seas.
Until now.

Unbecoming

Here and now shall we unveil you completely.
As this poet unveils you, and brings you naked to the
 council of the eyeless one.
See, there, I have nearly revealed too much.
I am the alien you fear,
And I proclaim my self as such...believe and think what
 you will.
Here I am, I stand so simply before you.
You are invisible in the midst of your kind.
You think I sleep in the dumpsters of your city.
You try to avoid my gaze.
I confront thee and demand that you answer...
What do I hear, on the hill, over the mountain, in the
 heart of summer nights?
So fierce they come like lumbering apes, taking what
 they desire,
Killing those who refuse their presence.
Silver birds and jellied fires rain from the sky, and there
 is no way to turn.
It sticks to your skin and eyes, and you vaporize where
 you stand.
Look with horror into the eye of the beast, for yours is
 not to act.
Your options are closed, predetermined.
Where now is your benevolent God?
Why isn't God watching?

There is no time to move your feet, the fire comes at you,
A red and white hurricane.
You gasp, and are burned to a crisp.
There is no time to feel pain, to say goodbye.
You are every mother, every child, every human who ever lived,
Who lived to die in the jelly gas
The chemical fires, and the atomics
Begotten beasts unleashed and nurtured by your scientists and politicians.
So gleefully you embrace and cajole them
Who define your horror, who hover over your dead children for the nation state,
And explain it for the sake of God.
Yes, vomit over this, while God is your shield.
You sit weakly and obedient, engaging these taxes like sheep.
You are the great, plodding, mindless goat.
This is the realm of the stupid, the land of the sleepers..
Enter the herd.
I would rid my self of you, but I cannot.
This is what I see over the great wide world.
Sweet children, and you who are preciously unborn,
I fear you are doomed.
The great wings of your mothers, the great wings of your fathers,
These very beings who spawned you, have you forever committed to their contrivances,
To the nightmare symphonies of national aggression, and the way of the good citizen.
The sun burns at billions of degrees, in it's pure atomic neutron fire,
The numbers are so large I cannot conceive of the quantities,
They are huge beyond imagining they are so immense.
The great, beautiful sun looks down and is ashamed.

In the ice of a forgotten winter,
One pink flower blossoms on the end of a twig.
I gaze out upon this flower, and feel the quiet snows fall.
They fall forever within.

Here You Are Now, My Poets

My beautiful poets, with your divine visions, your humanness.
Your stories of madness and equally the divine.
You are more rare than the grandest flower, the most spectacular storm.
You are precious gifts, concealed and often invisible to the populous you serve.
I weep for your greatness, for the one thing that you do.
I rage for your smallest word, line or quatrain...
We are the forthcoming poets, the terrible mirrors who reflect what is and is not.
We come and chronicle the ages of our kind.
We see the madness of the false ones, the shadow priests.

The dark riders and their false deities, their cloaked ministries,
Corrupt, festering servile beings.
Lavishly they praise and caress you, and with astonishing precision and coolness.
What is beautiful and green and full of life's precious energy is soon destroyed.
For the sake of God,
For the good of the nation,
For it is their manifest destiny, their eminent domain.
Golden eyed they stand before you, in polished suits
They recite scripted enchantments.

Dear poet, where are you going?
Have you seen enough?

Do you shudder under the futility and hopelessness of it?
Does your heart say "I can not go anymore along this way.
I my self will turn and become spoiled, and rot in my own stench."
It will not be clear at first, and once I am gone, it will be too late.
Do the crows of darkness consume your soul,
Does the vapid greater mind swarm and surround you?
Does the cool air you breathe become less with each inhale?
Is the rainbow darkening with the evening sky?
I beg thee, be strong.
I have saved all my stars for thee.
Become the circle in the spiral, the body electric,
You are the clear sighted and clean one.
This I have my self done, and continue to do.
Do you see that I am Wind In His Hair?
Do you see that I am your friend?
That I will always be your friend?

Fight the good fight of the ragged poet,
Go forth with your wooden spoon and your bowl.
Gather your soft, unpressed robes around you.
The rabble cannot dissuade you.
Go back to those who have gone before.
There you will find it again.
You will see the colors anew, the scents freshly broken.
The fog will become vital and fresh in your lungs, helping you to breathe.
The filth and stench of the pervasive world will fall and you will become luminous.
Find the diamond within, and let if flow,
Always keep the diamond in your mind.
Shine on my sisters and brothers.

Shine on Wolf Brother, Wind Sister, Ocean Lover, and
   Moon Goddess…

A world of nation souls awaits your deliverance.
The machine that opposes you is riddled with
   weaknesses.
It is a mind with no logic, only deceit, cunning, and false
   seductions.
It cannot withstand your onslaught.
It cannot bear the presence of what is pure and essential
   about you.
Hold this diamond in your mind's eye.
I present it to thee for your loving heart to cherish.
This I do for you, only because I love you, and all that
   you know or do,
I go before as your champion.
I make the path safe and known for only you to
   recognize.
I often linger in the shadow as you pass,
Quietly misdirecting those who might do you harm.
Ninja Poet, Samurai Poet, you only sense my presence,
When I choose, I pass unseen.

The Clowns Slowly Fade

The theater is still.
The moon shines white in the black, empty deep, and I
    go there.
There is peace and stillness in the face of the moon.
I float for a moment, and find my body is now upright in
    the cool sand.
The smell of salt brine and sea life fermenting in the
    tidal areas fills my lungs.
On a silvery light chain a small boat rests in the water,
Her nose to the wind, water slapping softly on her sides.

This is my boat,
I built it with the help of some friends.
She is strong, and as any sailor will tell you, she is a
    woman.
I have no explanation for this image.
Go to sea on a boat, and you will know.
You will know what I mean, and you will understand.
My boat, this vessel, is strong, but not too strong, small
    but sufficient.
She is supple, but not soft.
She shines, but she hides in the shadow.
She is full of power, and when necessary, invisible to
    those who would do us harm.
In this boat,
We go out on the ocean.
This is where we belong.
Away from the things of human beings, away from the
    civilized and the righteous,
Where clowns die.

As is widely known in the world of the stars,
Clowns do not know how to swim,
The high priests believe they will fall off the edge of the
    earth,
And their knowledge of boats is limited...
They will not eat the oysters of the sea.

The Ruling Class

Those who are oppressive among you,
Those who have acquired physical power and resources
    beyond their capacity,
In numbers and quantities so great the mind cannot
    grasp them intellectually,
You who continually feed and prey upon the less strong,
    the less resourceful.
You who cloak your selves in governments and ideologies
    and religions.
Those who acquire this advantage promote and build
    upon it,
Until their wealth is beyond numbers that a single
    human might count,
Beyond comprehension, like the fire of the sun.
Do you know what is contained in the quantity of one
    hundred, one thousand, one million, or more?
Is the palm of your hand sufficient?
Does it contain enough?
Have you eaten more than once this day?
You have wealth beyond your needs, perhaps a billion
    fold.
Does the stretch become apparent to you as you read
    these letters I place so orderly and lovingly before
    you?
In your world, in every moment of your history,
Living souls lie butchered,
Tortured and ripped to bloody pieces by your
    machineries of conquest and war.
What was my flesh is now the breeding ground for
    maggots.

We are the United States of Manifest Destiny,
Who seized with gunpowder and ballistics this great nation state.
We exterminated whole cultures of human beings,
And we replaced them with the knives of the Christian churches.
We marched forth with our holiness ablaze,
We drew imaginary lines in the sand and with imaginary words,
We invented concepts of common law, only words on paper for specialists,
Called them our own.

My dearest tribal wanderer,
Who now find your self and your people dissociated from the earth mother.
I am coming to find you in your many forms,
My romantic love is to be with you forever.
I am the ancient one, and I have always been by your side.
I am One Who Waits, and I am your brother.
I am equally your sister, and your mother and your father.
All that you are, this I am also.
Look deeply within your self.
You will find me there, and in every atom around you.

My only wish is to lie with you beside the wood fire at night,
At night under blankets of the worlds animals,
To live and breathe and watch the stars moving overhead.
Near to this stream, under the spreading green canopy of trees,
I come to lie naked and clean with you,
And roll with your body, over and over,

With our brothers and sisters, the sea otter,
And the mountain squirrel.
Your skin is smooth like the harbor seal, and I am crazy
 to touch it.
When the smell of the whites comes, we will quietly
 move away.
The yellow wolf beside us, will tell us when they are
 coming around.

I am shadow in the mountain.
The stars become the air, and with each breath I take,
It is then impossible that I am not breathing stars.
And with this stuff of the air, I pass through you,
As well as you pass through me.
Inside and out, I am the whole universe.
I may come near you in some city,
And somehow we may come into contact,
Even as pedestrians passing along some street or in a
 market or fragrant garden,
And you will know this.
You will know what I mean...

For The Landlords

Do you own the land?
Is the sea your property?
Who directs the winds, and the storms, and the warm
    shine of your nearest suns...
Does the Tsunami wave ask your permission?
Does it fill out forms for your approval?
Does the exploding volcano pause to acknowledge you?
Have you given notice to vacate?
You lack what is essential,
You are not significant.
Perhaps you are no more than the dirt beneath my feet.
Perhaps you are an illusion, a dream that fades and
    becomes as nothing?
My eyes grow sad and weary as I watch you.
The ages pass, and your weapons become more
    advanced.
You and your kind slowly become more clever.
Just as your mind control systems become more subtle
    and far reaching.
I am become the media, the destroyer of worlds.

What you call your governments, religions, and
    philosophies.
I see them in the bloody eyes of babies in Africa,
I see them in the piles of rent bodies that lie in the after
    fields and bogs of your killing days in Cambodia.
Each of your nation states goes forth, time and time
    again,
So fully certain, so completely justified, right in their
    own minds,

As the weapons of death strike the bodies, the beautiful supple limbs of your brothers and sisters, your mothers and fathers.
The sweet smooth skin of your children's children,
The deepest blue or brown or green or grey eyes of any one of them.

The Belly Of The Beast

All are fodder to the belly of war...
How many of the breathing animals of your planet feed
 upon themselves in this way?
I have seen the wolves. They hunt only for food.
They do not acquire trophies, or build fences on the land.
They are the genius that defines them.
They are the beauty you have lost.
These creatures, these beings, they are your teachers.
Take them as your soul and spirit guides.
They will do you only good,
And will ask nothing in return.

My sight diminishes as I slowly gaze over the rubble of
 your atomic weapons.
I gaze upon your methane and fire and jellied petroleum
 bombs.
I see the barbequed, charred flesh of screaming souls.
Minutes ago they were laughing and digging in their
 gardens.
Minutes before they were caressing each other in soft
 sheets and bedrooms.

On and on you go, one tyranny replaces another,
One madness evolves in form and the next battle is
 started.
Here is the essence of human ignorance, as well as it's
 stupidity!
How far we have come, how advanced and great is the
 human species!

It's greatest failing over the thousands of years, the
    countless time, the eons.
You fail to see the horror of your acts and change your
    way.
You continue to praise and congratulate upon your great
    successes and accomplishments.
Where is your love and compassion for another?
Where does it go?
You gather the resources of the earth, the fortunes of
    kings.
And you squander it on murdering each other.
You breed and sustain the under classes to do your
    labors
You tax them to fill your coffers and the bank accounts
    of the gentry
You who are the ruling classes.
And when one generation has lost its memory,
When the horror is diminished and faded,
You cloak yourselves in God and righteous rhetoric,
And you begin anew.
The Juggernaut...

You create specialized languages that become your
    justifications,
Your road maps for control and the exercise of terror.
Your laws, your governances, your taxes that create
    unlimited wealth.
For those of the ruling classes.
You are the modern Necromancers, spinning spells and
    casting potions of deception.

My Brother, My Sister

Brother Wind, Sister Moon, carry me!
Without you I am nothing!
In your absence, I would simply retreat, and become the
    nothing that is my essence!
I stand on the far hillside, and hold the weathervane
    aloft!
It is for you to see!
It is for you to carry forth, and open the vaults of
    madness!
Take my ideas to the fools of this earth,
Take me out and shake me before them!
Strip the blood and senses from my body until they
    understand, until I am gone for good! I know it is
    sad for you to think this,
But a day may come when I will no longer show my self
    in this place!
Act now while there is still time, for time there is,
But not forever as many think!
May the stupid become wise!
The foolish are easy to find!
They are everywhere you look!
Everywhere you go!
If you are not careful, you may actually be touching one
    in this moment that I hold you!

Now, who am I, you say?
Who comes forth so boastful, so arrogant, so positive and
    wise?
Who is this greybeard? Some bard of olden time, some
    ancient wizard?

Is he the Merlin, the Leonardo, the Fool on the Hill, the
    Old Walt newly born again?
I am borne of the stars, and there I dwell!
In vain they pursue me!
I am One Who Waits!
Look for me! I have come for you, and for you alone!
I am the magician who enlightens by revealing!
Do not be ashamed!
I see your body and the soul it contains and so I love
    thee...
Come to my tent this night, and I will show you!

Under the dark clear winter sky of the northlands, look
    up, and see there what is undeniable!
I am what you will never misconceive!
I present so obvious and formidable before you!
Do not 'err as the others, who fear they have seen a
    ghost, or are in the presence of some demon!

I am for your mind and also for your heart!
With me you shall ever ride, ride upon the wind!
The astral winds!
The winds of space and time,
And whatever composes their essence as well!
Do you think we have seen to the final element?
Your destiny will not allow you to do otherwise.
You know what I say, and that I am true,
You sense already that I know you, know your soul, and
    just what is essential?
Nothing more, and nothing less...

Your way is clear, dear companion,
I cannot tell you how to go.
But I can promise you this, in the simple and pure
    language,
In the plain text and words of friends,

I am, and will always be with you.
I am Wind In His Hair,
Do you know that I am your friend?
Do you know that I will always be your friend?

The Time Is Now

Come then, is this the time?
Is this the moment in which we believe?
Do all the great poets gather 'round and beseech thee?
Is this Walt, the Old Greybeard, the singular bard
    singing his song of the self?
Has my soul come down from the mountain and finally
    said unto me:
Awaken and sing!
I must be continuing, conjoined with those gone before!
For there is no time left?
Hoards of the spirits of the past present themselves,
They reach from dark maddening places,
Pressing their bony fingers into my flesh,
Pulling me forward to greet this moment,
Having spent so long in waiting.

I see them!
Now I understand, and I come for you,
You who wonder at my meaning also,
Who think of nothing special each waking day,
You who are forever numbed by the myriad narcotic
    pastes and potions of your culture.

Break me now, and open what I reveal for thee as sweet
    cream and essences...
Behold the vague departing visions of the old mystics
    and seers who roam the world, Who wander
    cloaked in their magic robes, transparent, and
    dreamlike,

Unsettling to the jaded, leering eyes of the festering, sickened populous.
I sometimes fear they come less often.

This I tell you in complete confidence and with absolute certitude,
That we are the mighty giants of the soul, of the true self, the individual.
The experience that eludes the common ones,
The anemic bloodless corpses that pass everywhere for the living.

Shoulder Your Duds Dear One

Do you sense what I am about?
Is there an itch within you that speaks forth with the same demanding urgency?
Drop your shroud, dear companion, take up your staff and cloak!
Come lightly! You have no time for the burden of wealth or great possessions.
We travel the road lightly afoot,
Ready to change our pursuit at the moment's notice, if need be.
Others will come pursuing with false intentions,
We must be prepared to step aside and let them pass.
They would harm and oppress what is finest about us.
You, the soul of the beautiful woman, and you, the soul of the beautiful man!

Come my comrade, my child, my parent, come travel with me!
I am ready for you, and will love you as no other has loved you before,
Or will ever love you again!
My love is true, once established, and will never diminish.
Trust in this, if you believe nothing else I say!
I will do you good, and you will find shelter from the storm!
Stand forth with me on the prow of this great ship,
Let the sting of the salt spray douse you until we stand soaking wet.

Indeed, you will become your self the storm that
 confronts you!
Proceeding in this manner, you will ride the dragon,
You will find that all is consumed in your path.
Indeed, you will find you are become the one,
The one who is all things, the destroyer and the creator!
And I will become your lover, the sweet, sweet rose...

Coming This Way I Caution You...

You will at times find your self in shadow,
Pursued by a sprightly ghost that shrinks and fades in pale, twilit forms,
You will fear what you see before you and what you come to know.
Your soul will consume it's self in terror.
At night, you will become the darkness, and there will be nothing to relieve you.
What you think is your self, established, firm, confident, strident and unwavering, will become as nothing.
An endless abyss will swallow the illusion of you,
And you, my friend, will know and become horror,
Beyond the fullest imagining of this term.
You will find and understand the precursor to the roots of all language and thought,
The beast will gaze upon you.
What will come next, cannot be told,
Cannot be communicated in this primitive manifestation we call language.

Will You Meet Me There?

Will you abandon all your prior forms and enter this place with me?
Do you have in hand your cup, your staff, and a stout knife?
Do I recognize upon your face now the smile of the great bards of old, the lusty poets who seduce us while we sit and drink at the weathered road houses of eternity?
This, my port of departure, where I turn slowly with some sadness, some regret.
Where I glow forever like the fiery sun, some whirling comet, some evolving galaxy or yet to be known particle of unknown substance or origin?

Of course, it must be so!
We are easily within reach!
Take my hand now for we must be off,
There are no more delays, no goodbyes,
No loving touches to the flesh that was once yours!
Linger no more on the shore, or you are lost!
Do you see?
It is your time!
Seize it with all your strength, you have it within you!
And, do you see!
There on the hill, someone waits for you,
Turning but a moment to look over his shoulder, in his comfortable old coat, and high-top shoes, with eyes that glow like stars in the winter sky...
He seems to point, like a weather vane, just over the next hill...

A Short Walk

There is a coolness in the bricks,
Softly singing like old birds under my feet as I float toward the bay in old town.
Green water fills the air and sky,
I flex my thighs and hips to the rhythm of something,
Some thing oozing around my head, floating over the earth with no feet,
Really no direction, no sound of others.
Mist defines the boundaries of the world.
Beyond definition, comprehension,
I turn around the blue light of the hedges where the dogs lurk quietly,
Smoke rolling from their nostrils,
Heating the night, like orange candle eyes,
Sniffing my fingers for food or sex or wonder.
Who are these dogs, I think?
Wanderers, random and lusty, bleeding for God.
Fuck them. My heavy black boots thump softly as I turn away,
Continuing on down the paved roads and sidewalks,
The damp night air moving in eddies throughout my long overcoat,
Cooling me and carrying away the moist vapors of my body.
Approaching from down the street,
A bundle of darkness slowly spews thick steam from its hood.
Clouds of autumn rustle my hips from under,
Twinkling angels collide in my chest, as it comes closer to me.

But far away, and vague still, no ideas, no substance.
Feeling in my pocket the damp material and earth smells
I inhale slowly and turn a complete circle within.
Slight sounds from the feet of her,
I see now that it is female and bundled well against the night...so dark the night.
The face is buried, a dark cavity in the thick swathing of cotton and wool,
Slow bursts of damp air emerge in strange cadence as we drift nearer
And resolve the evening to collide like great ships.
The purple and green hues of the night shimmer off her clothing,
Perhaps these are tiny stars reflecting or emitting from somewhere deep within her.
My heart pulses briefly, reminding me of it's presence.
And some other subtle signal flickers through me.

Sitting on a bench overlooking the bay and old homes of this port city,
I inhale the smoky night,
Closing me deeper, sea smells and fog.
The surreal figure approaches from my left,
Pausing to exhale and smoke the night air , panting and still, wet and powerful.
"Good evening" emerges from her Cheshire mouth,
Ripples of water and glimmering icicles cause me to shift,
Although sensing an ethereal likeness between us,
As if trapped in some ancient spell or incantation.
Now I am soaring over Egypt,
The dry dust of time covers the land,
The great pyramids look out over the vast empty desert.
I turn once,
I am back,

She comes close to me.
Don't say anything, if that's all you can say.
"Hello" I speak, somehow, with great effort.
"Nice night?" questioningly indifferent to her.
"I don't know" she replies. It sounds so constrained, yet
 musical.
She knows something, the dreams are touching I think.
"Sit with me for a while?" I say softly. "The view over the
 water is magical"
And, thinking to my self, we are certainly for each other.
She is dark and moves quietly,
Balanced, dancing in the still cocoon of her coat and
 boots.
I feel moist air rolling down my throat, filling my chest
 and belly.
She moves toward me and extends her fingers to touch
 my shoulder,
Snow on the mountain...

Stars glitter on the huge water of the bay below us,
Quieting our thoughts and voices,
We are little Buddha, little Bodidharma, touching and
 not touching.
High in the mountains, somewhere over China, a bird
 reels and floats,
Disappearing in blue and white.
Wonderful, she knows the ancient ways, touches without
 words,
Caresses with dreams and stillness.

Years pass and I turn to her, my leg pressed against her
 heavy clothing.
She leans in and presses back, smiling slightly and for
 the first time that I can tell.
Fumes of her body reach around me as I relax in her
 nature,

A feminine aura envelopes me.
Yes, there is a difference between men and women.
The musk of the night air is rich and powerful,
The gentle pressing and releasing of her body harmonizing,
Rustling with the fall leaves, through tumbling, swirling moonbeams.
I draw closer to her face, shrouded still in the blue and gray hood,
I see the smooth rich lines of her skin, coolly radiant and beautiful.

The street lamps glow like rainbows under the thick canopy of maple trees.
One hand slowly touches the cheek of her face,
Close now to engaging and mingling the breath from our lungs,
Molding our shapes together, lips touching, fully embracing, warm necks together, Holding strongly.
I dream the gulls are crying, because they are hungry,
Because they are dying.
The full wet contact now of her lips on my lips,
Opening our mouths at once with dancing tongues lightning and electric.
Shivering, we close together, combining as mighty rivers on some wild journey to a distant sea.
I become thee, in this moment on the escarpment,
I am the face of Bodidharma.
I am the face of all Gods, and of no Gods,
Every Buddha, and every divine concept ever dreamed in the language mind reality of anyone, or anything.
I have no explanation for this.
No thing exists above, below or beyond this moment,

You show me the faceless roar of eternity, you who are
    the fire and ice.
Wing me to the snow bound wilderness of your mind's
    eye,
The breaking awareness of all things constant and ever
    changing.
You, my vortex, consume me.
Dragon emerges from the never ending skies.
I have not eaten this day...

We stumble toward the cool bluer ocean, the rolling,
    rocking, undulating bay.
The cobblestone shifts and slither under our feet,
Giant timbers of old homes groaning like dead schooners
    on the sea bottom.
Moss covers the stone way as we thread the back alleys,
Avoiding the dogs and their strange snuffling noises.
Soft night surrounds us.
We embrace as if we had traveled together for a
    thousand years.
She is strong and of the earth, pushing her hips into my
    hips,
We separate and we part, our flesh closing together and
    then opening,
Penetrating and blending like watery fountains.
The wind runs over my back, like the sea otter down a
    grassy slope.
Scents and shadows call us on through the old
    neighborhood,
Scurrying through the darkness underfoot,
Balancing on the slimy moss growing over the old red
    stonework of the cobbled roadways,
Curving up and down in irregular humps, tripping us as
    we go.
We are nothing to this.

I fly as my body is gone now, and this is our spirit ride
 and no thing stands before us.
No limit is conceived.
The sun is the moon and all the known stars are
 openings to new worlds.
We glide, borne of the earth and water,
Cradled and pursued by the natural ways of magic and
 wizards.
We stroll the paths of the night together, warm with
 each others thoughts,
Cool with the universe, feeling the bodies of our selves
 and not our selves,
Reeling into the arms of October angels,
Full tongues and lips sliding in and out,
Over each other, the pure light of stars in our eyes.

The old stadium grounds loom in the darkness,
Concealing long hidden places.
Ghosts and dead children whisper as we pass under the
 monstrous gray spires and ramparts.
Here, I think, is paradise.
On we go, the soil wet and slick beneath us,
The mist a shroud of comfort and secrecy.
Soon we are on the high bank where the train tracks cut
 into the hillside
And go on forever.
On one hip she rests one hand, the weight pulling me in
 to her lightly.
Deeply I reach and the thick layers of cloth open to my
 exploring fingers,
Finding their way into and over her skin,
She yields and conforms to my lightly nervous, quivering
 touches.
Stand and forget the world in common,
Open to this dream and it will be you and yours alone,
 until time goes no more.

Until past, present and future become the singularity,
    the Eschaton.

Shifting into the bulk of her coat
My hands reach to the waistband of her outer pants and
    find the material yields easily,
I glide my fingers gently over the flesh of her full white
    belly,
Shuddering at the cool touch,
Gentle protocols giving way to more urgent and primal
    sensations.
Her shirt tails pull out, up and away from her waist,
Her torso firm and smooth and thick,
Flexing and bowing as I find the white mounds of her
    breasts
Touching the pointed red prominences .
They are hard and alive in my fingertips,
I roll them under and over themselves,
She gasps and twitches, breathing deep and long,
    opening inside.
She closes her eyes, in some rapturous trance ...

My hips graze over the softness of her belly, probing
    with primal intelligence.
I am the firewalker, spinning in place, breathing more
    slowly now,
Poised and stepping lightly.
She finds my eyes, crying, as our bellies heave together,
The cloth of her shirt rumpled and warming my hands,
We are wrapped in our combined cloaks, slowing the
    circle now.
Kissing deeply, tasting her mouth,
I ease again into her waistband, free of shirt tails,
Thick, hard fingers revealing her flesh and warmth.
I penetrate lower, moving to the moist slipperiness
    between her thighs,

Her opening yields the body electric,
Conjoined as binary stars.

The weight of her compressed with my own,
Two arms pulling on mine, pulling me in,
We separate slightly, eyes scanning the night,
Breathing again as we had become one body, one mind,
 one soul.
"We are one" she sighs.
With swollen wet lips, her full, long fingers and hands
 arousing me,
Some essence of who we were warming in the dark, blue
 sea air.
Long overcoats hang loosely around us,
Like small Bedouin tents, blending the cool of air of the
 night with our bodies.
The fingers of my left hand hold the tight flesh of her
 bottom,
Feeling and probing gently, pulling her open,
Exposing the tightness of her opening to the cool air.
Sharp, sudden breath hisses over me, lusty and deep.
I feel it the same.
We sway from side to side, one with our breathing,
 harmonic in the *uberspricht*.
Ringing and moving the center of her,
Softly massaging her muscle,
Rushing forward, falling as dream bodies in a suddenly
 thrilling, abyssal darkness.
She presses imperceptibly backward, urging me in.
Forms become light, with intense pleasure.
New and rushing stars emerge in our combined mentat,
Playing to the scarecrow music of the dark carnivals of
 October.
We hear far and away the odd cadence and noises of
 harvest storms,

Filled with strange languages not often repeated to the children of earth.
Dropping to my knees I smell her deeply, profoundly,
Clutching her hips to my face, pressing and rotating.
Like the dreaming great fishes of the ocean,
She clamps full around me, bucking and extending her body,
Convulsing and spending liquid down her legs into my opening mouth.
In and out now, slowly, like a summoned demon,
Trees rustle low around the pool of our beings, like evening rain.
Weightless, it seems I am suspended in her,
With her, floating, no universe, no backing up,
I cannot move forward, light shimmers from all directions,
All is peaceful and serene, euphoric.
She bucks strongly now at my face with her hips sliding over and over,
My tongue reflexively pushes into her, my hand clenched by her hips,
And locked by the muscular contractions.
I am the wolf, and never saw the trap...

What once were perhaps our bodies,
Now transform to liquid, easing to the soft earth,
Consumed and still, thrusting slowly,
Squatting over the mass of cloaks and flesh I see the million faces of her,
Faces of us, reeling kaleidoscopes of our lives past, present and future.
One hand reaching into my pants,
Holding the thickness, pumping me tight and with slow deliberation.
The wonder of this, the ecstasy of touching.

How do worlds and constructs deny it's purity and essential nature?
You who fear the body, and deny the soul.
Arching my back the night returns briefly,
The muted darkened shapes appear again in more expected configurations.
Human residences, commercial buildings,
Cloaked in their stones and woodwork sway imperceptibly on engineered foundations. Leaning my eyes skyward, I become unbalanced, powerful.
I caress myself smoothly and look again upon the body of this other.
She is beauty and fire, ice and myst,
She is far and away, and yet so near.
Her luminous white breasts heave and twitch.
She is slowing now, releasing my hand from her, easing out gently.
Her round bottom caresses my finger, as I slide out and away.

She smiles enigmatically, shifting in her bed of blue and gray cloth.
I hover astride and athwart her hips, our minds opening and closing like jellyfish,
We are penetrating spirits, carnival souls.
Blue diamonds flicker and glow,
Easing down over her,
Dragging across the cool marble of her thighs,
Blood engorged and strong, soft and female.
My slick emission trails over her skin, oozing slowly,
Sticky and dripping.
Flexing under me, pulling her thighs up close to her chest,
She exposes the purple and red flesh of her opening.
Enticing me, splaying her legs wide,

My thighs rub over the exposed back of her legs and
    buttocks.
I ease forward, and the thick, heavy flesh between my
    legs draws back and forth over her pubic mound.
Some universal constant overtakes our minds,
The two of us show the one of us.
Slipping in fully with bellies pressed tightly,
Exhaling, pressing her insides open to wrap me,
My tongue thrusting the air, finding the sweetness of
    our lips and mouths.

"Never" she says "were we like this."
Flesh tingling, rippling fireflies, rolling onto our backs,
The hillside under us warm and wet, we gently dream.
Who are you there, in the shadow?

Mon Sheri

I have seen her once since 1977?
I never stop trying to reach her.
I think I did once or twice, but she never calls back.
She was sitting on a state ferry to Bainbridge Island once
Leaving the Coleman Dock in Seattle.
I was with a psychotic, abusive man-hater from the east coast named Margaret.
Do not ask me how I got there.
It is a long, sad story.
It happened so long ago,
Long before the time of my becoming unstupid.
I become unstupid one starry night on the Quinault River,
Burning a Druid fire on Inner Creek, with Bodi, my long haired American Dingo.

I sat down in an open booth and there she was.
In the next booth, a couple of seats over, next to the window.
She was with what was apparently her family,
An older couple, a couple of young bratlings, and a man closer to her age.
I was frozen and my heart started to pound.
My voice and mind were stolen.
Probably her in-laws.
I have met her father, and would have recognized him.
Her mother died years before from cancer.

It was during this time of her mother's re-emerging
 illness that my friend and lover sort of went south
 on me.
And I pretty much just watched her go.
I could not speak, and got up to go into the men's room,
 the only immediate escape.
I wanted to blurt out her name, but I was with the
 psycho-bitch,
I did not want to shame, embarrass or surprise anyone.
What an odd thing to feel.
For years I had tried to make contact with her through
 her family,
Through phonebooks,
Through late nights with whiskey and the long distance
 operator, and etc.
Now, just like in a storybook, she was close enough to
 touch.
Now, all of a sudden I was a bashful 19 year old,
 standing in the hallway,
Afraid to breathe.
Maybe this was excitement,
Maybe this is part of how you are when you love with
 intensity, with profundity.
When I came out from my escape to the head,
She was moving toward the front of the boat with her
 group, and I said nothing.
I did nothing.
I stood and watched her slowly walk away.
Shortly after I did find Sheri's number in the phone
 listings.
She was practicing clinical psychology in Gatesville.
I called and left messages, but they were never returned.
I drove by her office once or twice, but never went in.
I am too embarrassed.
I am the dumb shit.
The fool on the hill...

Sheri is all I ever combined into the most singular love of
 my life…perhaps my true companion.
I don't even remember if I am spelling her name
 correctly.
Sherri or Sheri? Or was it Sherry?
She was a female form of me, in divine purity and
 beauty.
I try to recall clearly the first day I saw her.
I think I can, but am not so sure.
It was a classroom in Bellingham Washington,
We both were enrolled at a small public college there we
 all called Western.
Maybe it was between classes, in the hall, or Red
 Square,
Or on some rainy night going back to my dormitory
 room.
I had already spent time there at an experimental annex
 known as Fairhaven.

How I ever got up the nerve to first confront and speak
 to her,
Will forever be beyond my comprehension.
Probably it was she that first approached,
And said something naturally simple and pleasant,
Sensing my terror and apprehension.
We did come together somehow, it turns out,
And I will think of Sheri, always, as the most perfect
 woman for me,
My Comerado, as Old Walt might say.
That we would share four brief years together,
And drift apart quietly, gently, and for no good reason,
Will haunt me until the day I die.

Even now, I find my self turning, expecting to see her next to me.
Sometimes, she is there.
Really.
As lovely and radiant as always,
Boring into me with her dark, intelligent brown eyes and smiling sweetly.
Sometimes I feel her, and I don't just mean in some allegoric sense.
I mean, I really feel her.
I feel her palm, moist against mine,
Her fingers are strong and squeezing my hand tightly
As if to say "It is your fate now, Gary, never let us drift apart.
Keep me here, against all others, and fight for me against the others you know will come pursuing me."
This is what I did not do.
Let go of that which you most cherish and adore.
This is the way of the enlightened ones.
If you truly love something, you must let go of it. I said, let go of it...
She remains my goddess, my transfigured one,
She taught me the essence of Namaste.
There is some literal, scriptural translation, I am sure,
But here is my concept of it, sitting here now,
Looking over the cool waters of Commencement Bay
From my small massage therapy treatment room:
When the divine presence within me abandons the small petty things of the world, and recognizes the divine presence within you, and the divine presence within you abandons the small petty things of the world and recognizes the divine presence within me, then we shall meet as one in complete joy and harmony.

This is what Sheri means to me, still, to this day,
At least in some garbled but loving form of it.
As words may be the final reality,
As linguistic conceptualizations may be all that causes
    our self awareness,
I cannot be sure.
Who do I look like, Einstein?
Surely, no matter what,
If some unknown comet should come by
Suddenly to hurl the completely holy shit out of me,
I will find what is left shimmering in some dark corner
    of the universe,
What I was in the mind of this woman.
Who touched me in subtle and obvious ways,
And in the most profound of all ways,
And who kept the vague and powerful existential horror
    at bay,
At least for a while.

These shrouds I cherish,
These remnants of times and days and nights that live
    forever,
As long as I live, anyway...
As long as this mind conceives memories of happy,
    exhilarating moments,
The wonder and warmth of a touch,
The grazing of skin against skin,
Cheek to cheek,
The rapture of passion shared in damp bed sheets
And in couplings on the sandy ocean beaches of the
    Pacific.

I miss you bright eyes, my wonderful Indian spirit
    woman.
I sit on this hilltop, high in the clouds,

And the blue and white reflections of the sky loom on the
    horizon.
Hovering in this body of light, cross legged,
I know I am floating,
That I am above the earth and rocky slopes.
And that I see both inward and outward,
Slowly expanding, and here now,
This hand rests comfortably on your thigh,
And the sky goes on forever, beyond the four corners,
We are seated side by side,
On this eternal carnival ride,
We are flowing through eternity,
Smiling in our knowing hearts,
And not knowing anything, becoming all moments and
    events.
How I have died the death of a million suns,
And known the quiet luminous birth of one silent moon,
In you, my dearest darling young one.
From one who has nothing to offer,
And even less to give,
I have saved all my stars for thee...

Romantic Western Love

It comes from within.
I have loved many people, many women, with great intensity.
Powerfully, and with abandon.
Many of these women actually proclaimed there love for me.
They are all gone now.
Not dead, that I know, just gone.
Gone on to their subsequent intense loves, lives and activities.
One or two I have contacted after some many years passed.
Love is forever, or maybe just for eighteen months or so.
Until the next best thing comes along.
Until I no longer do what you say.
Until my body no longer suits you.
There is a powerful energy within me.
I think it is romantic western love.
I think there are many women in the universe.
I think when I combine them all into one,
When all that is love remains,
When all that is deception, disappointment and pain falls away,
Then I will know my true companion.
And she will dwell forever in my heart,
And she will become one in my soul, and I to her the same.
This day, this singular moment will come, and will come again.
Love is the myriad kaleidoscope of all that is within me,

It is conceived in the language of joy and wonder I
 create.
Love is all the women I have known,
When the madness and scorn are stripped away,
When the lies, deceit, and pettiness glimmer and fade,
Love shimmers within, is an archetype,
I love you, I will always love you.
When I say this, believe me...
Whoever you are?

Looni Bird

Open me! This you gasp in a half desperate whisper,
Half sitting up on the table where you are before me naked.
Your tiny hands, strong and grasping,
In your frantic way, took hold of my hands,
Large and strong, thick and engorged with blood from rubbing you.
I make deep, large circles in your flesh,
Stand over you, caressing you,
Moving into your soft white belly,
And as you grasp me, you press into my wrists,
You direct me further downward along your smooth torso,
Resting over the roundness of your pubic mound,
Where light blond curls grow and glisten with body oil and moisture.
You press into my hands, your breath coming fast and more shallow with each movement
Each upward thrust of your small, powerful pelvis.
So blue those eyes, so white this smile,
So sweet the smell and musk of your presence,
The erotic grinding of your groin and thighs,
Your hips vibrating urgently to my slow, deepening touch,
The rasp of your breathing, encloses me.
Am I truly in this moment?
Will this lovely dream pass and turn foul or mundane?
No, you are real, you were there, and the love you expressed was direct.
This I know. I know it in the soul of my soul,

One Who Waits

From the deepest place where denial is futile.
Deeper now, deeper we go,
A shimmer comes back to me from some deep recess.
This is it.
Again I will pass into passion and boundless flight with
    another walker,
Another walker in the storm,
Here I see you, another fragrant and distant soul,
Gliding from some unknown land,
Swelling the sea of souls before us as we approach and
    touch,
One in this instant, and complete.
I know you, and have always known you,
As you have known me, and will always know me.
This is our fortune, our delight.
Without it, we shrivel and turn pale, as discarded rose
    petals neglected in the garden.
I love you, if only for this moment, this poem that we
    are.
You may deny what is me, what you perceive is me.
But you forever will not deny our song, our poetry.
It will gaze back at you as long as you live.
I am the terror and joy,
I am the greatest poet of all times, and you are fortunate
    to have found me.
Fear not, I ask nothing from you.
Only what is here in these moments, what passes for
    many as time,
Is the constant crystalline presence of our being.
Of our humanness.

Firmly now, but gently and lovingly,
I press you back down on the table with my one hand.
Last night, your man husband lay upon this same table.
Tomorrow morning he says, my wife will come to see
    you.

We are on holiday with our children.
This was her idea.
I tell this man, I came here to live my dream,
To abandon money and houses and petty fortunes.
How I wish I could do the same, he says.
There is till time, I assure him.
There is always time, as time is the illusion of western
    physicists and mathematicians.
You are not required to accept the concept.
Outside the window, the rain forest blew like soft snow.
I thought how unlike your bodies are.
He was thick and hairy, you so slight and smooth, like a
    water creature.
A million times a million of myriad events rush into my
    garden of Zen,
My center, my point - no point, the one point,
As I considered what was transpiring,
What was this, what are we really saying?
What are we and why?
Has every path become concealed and unknown to me?
Is this my fate alone?
But there is no comfort, no rationale in logic.
Constructs of language and the pseudo-mind of humans,
They float before my mind's eye with trivial banality.
There is no outcome, no idea, and no explanation.
The cool pinkish white cream of your half-raised thigh,
This and these things alone, they are reason enough.
And these I devour and consume, and you in turn, with
    your animal noises,
And the fastidious shuddering of you, as we become the
    one,
We become this moment, together,
And all that is false, that was an appearance, flows
    away, ungathering it's self,
And we dwell there, beyond the veil.

This perpetually vanishing moment will never be again,
It has no source, no destination, no genesis and no
    corollary.
Only the wonder and beauty of this real thing,
As it presents to our field of experience,
And to us, in this moment,
We fell and tumbled in the world of sprites and elves and
    fairies,
Where magic is the inexplicable moment, is every
    moment, and the call is obvious.

My thick hands encircle and cup your groin,
The moist hairy contour flexing, as you buck up to meet
    me.
Your arms push down hard against my cupped fingers,
You draw my hand up inside, filling you as I fist it up, as
    you insist I fill you,
Throwing back your head and squealing,
Your breathing becomes more and more staccato.
Do not stop, you insist, put more inside of me, and get
    bigger, harder.
We move together, in perfect harmony,
Each rhythmic stroke improving and building one upon,
    one inside, one within the other. On and on we
    moved, progressing out of time, reeling in galaxies
    light years away,
And still conscious, here in this cool, dark room,
In the dusky spring twilight of the rain forest.

Bending forward at my hips and slightly down,
I suckle as orgasmic juices flow from inside of you,
You bounce up and down on the soft padded table,
My face rising and falling with each movement,
I grasp around your thighs to keep us pressed in this
    urgent contact.

Your thighs rise completely into the air,
I chew lightly on the inner flesh of your vaginal lips with
    my teeth,
You urge me on and you scream,
I muzzle your mouth with my free hand
I feel you grab the edge of my pants,
Pulling the elastic waistband violently away,
In the love of humans, the reason we are in human
    forms,
You rub all over your face, mouth and your crotch.
Your tongue comes out of your mouth and you eat the
    fluid like it is your food.
I like this and watch it.
We become completely bathed and covered in our faces
    and sex organs,
Slick and sticky with these bodily juices and expulsions.
Slowing, we remain embracing and rocking,
I hold you and you hold me and we are one holding each
    other,
The juices of our sex glue us together.
Moving slowly, you reach up for some clean towels,
You bathe me with warm water and soap from the sink,
You sponge bathe our bodies,
Sometimes you find some still wet fluids,
This you clean with your fingers, swallowing and
    smiling,
You put some in my mouth,
And you kiss me,
Now you pinch my groin and testicles with your
    fingernails.
Juices ooze from me, as I flex with pain.
Pleasure overcomes, and so you, my soul, my smile, my
    heart, my mind.
I come to you in terror.
I am no longer free to go my own way.

Here, in this fresh, new gateway of my self and my
    conscious existence,
You came and showed me something as never before,
So terrifying and beautiful.
Now we are become this wonder, this wonderful thing.
Fare thee well, my dearest darling young one!
May you go with peace, and find love wherever you turn!
Know that I am with you!
When you look out upon the setting sun,
With pinkish blue skies and warming winds,
Know that I too look upon the same setting sun!
As the lightning strikes, and the storm rises, and your
    hair stands out on your neck,
Perhaps I sit beside you, as a specter or in some spirit
    form,
And lovingly place my hand upon yours,
Encircling your tiny fingers with my big fat ones,
And I and this thing that is my self take joy in simply
    being beside you.
We two, looking upon the setting sun…
In a farther world,
Remote and isolated,
On the drifting ice,
A tiny northern dingo sits and howls beneath the stars…
He calls to his brother, the wind,
He calls to his sister, the moon,
He is Bodi.
He is known to the elder tribes only,
He is One Who Waits.
He is my brother.

My Sweet Cold Ocean

Oh, my ocean! My sweet cold ocean!
Who becomes thee in the darkening afternoon, who joins
 you in your song?
Now I slowly walk, and here is this ghost hand in mine,
This hand of one I loved, and loved with the greatest
 passion.
Strange and remote you now seem to me.
Are you the spirit and essence of her?
Do you reflect her, and those loves from before, from all
 times perhaps?
Does this terrified lone poet seek you for this
 accumulation of souls you contain?
Here, I turn now again and she is gone.
The empty, solitary song of you pervades the night and
 completes me.
The gulls are circling, dropping shells and oysters in the
 sand...
They crack loudly when they open.

Breathing

If ever I do anything that offends thy presence,
Or in the slightest nuance of some subtle mannerism
I should without knowledge slight you in the smallest
    way.
Know that I would send life cryingly out of me,
And knowingly hurl my self only
Into some forever dream of the darkest abyss...
This I would gladly do.
There I will joyfully go.
To know simply that you breathe,
That you smile easily upon your children,
That you are cradled in the warm spring rain.
I go crazily picking buttercups,
I ask the spirit of the wind to carry them,
Gently one day to fall upon your beautiful sleeping eyes,
And there to melt forever...

The Rain Forest

Crouched in the high canopy of the forest,
She scans the lower places,
Clinging to branches in the low light of dusk, imagining strange vistas.
Orange and black beats her heart,
Halloween dreams of you.
One lies quietly on the still sand of the cove,
Eyes staring upward lazily, seeing inward more than out,
Warming like the tidelands in summer.
The cool rustling of leaves overhead, for an instant, becomes louder,
I orient toward the darkening woods of the island.
Something unknown flickers like a candle,
Glimmering rainbows appear undulating like great curtains suspended from the stars.
Dwell in constant wonder, perceive what lies beyond.
Know without knowing...
Something is in the forest, watching and waiting,
It is seething with life, touching my dream state.
From so far its eye shines.
I know it, I am with it, and understand what it knows.
There is another world in this thing, some dimension I missed.

I hear it singing and swaying in the branches like a monkey,
Yet more powerful and sinister.
My hand falls to the sand still warm from the evening sun,

Loving the earth sister who yields to my touch.
It seems so pointless to rise, so much energy for nothing.
In a dream I turn, peer into the darkening beauty and terror of the high canopy.
So many paths lead into the deep green leaves
The swirling smells of the living, rotting forest.
Blue night surrounds the sandy bay,
Strange birds flutter overhead uttering nonsensical phrases.
How did I get to this island?
No, this is no fair question.
I know the answer to this,
I came here my self, by my self, to be by my self.
And so nice it is, to finally be away from the babble, the rabble of the world.
How inane they seem to me.
Over time, it just got worse.
The more I try to think of them as cute darling children, the more pitiful they become. The harder it becomes to sit or walk among them.
They step on your feet, have no sense of grace or humility.
They horse around, acquiring things,
Acquiring symbols and great tracts of land
Representative icons of their wealth,
Their accomplishments, their great intelligence,
How their children got to the honor roll?
What the fuck is that?

After Midnight

Why don't you shave your head?
You would be even more striking that way.
Such a beautiful face, stands alone, like a new galaxy. I will do it for you, if you like!
Have fun on stage.
I did that during high school, at a coffee house in Tacoma.
I agree, the experience can be uncomfortable all around...
I do compose things.
I rarely write them down, but am always trying to remind my self to do that.
I have a document started, called The Opium Smoker.
At least for now, that may change.
A collection of prose and haiku style word images.
Short, powerful....
Remind me when you are here, you can read it.
It gets erotic.
You are the body electric...
When I kiss your mouth, my tongue will find you...

the color blue

Once, I fell into the sun,
All that I was became nothing,
Now I am unknown,
I breathe, I sit, I watch, I wait.

two women

Settled in a rhythmic stride, we slalom through the late afternoon coolness, like reptiles in steel. The little Ford Mustang hisses quietly over the blacktop of the river road, while the vast expanse of the Pacific Ocean looms in my thoughts. Trees wander by in the slanting, dappled light, appearing to shift places in green and blue ripples, taking us slowly toward the western coast. I can't think of its name. I should know the name of my star. I argue with my self. But then again, one should never consider anything seriously. Consider things distractedly, from a distance, remote and detached like a Buddha.

We are headed for Long Beach, Washington to rendezvous with Nikki and Jim. Nikki is Heather's girl friend from high school and Jim, is my old friend from high school. We are nearly a generation apart in age, as Heather was 16 years younger than I when we met at the Hanford Nuclear Site, where we both worked for the Department of Energy. She was a chemical engineer, and she had no idea what the chart of the elements was, had never ever seen it. Go figure...

Jim and I were acid buddies in high school during the late 60's, which took us sort of through the glory days of Gordon Wasson, Timothy Leary, and, incidentally, Vietnam. The bittersweet end of it. I was closer to her parents age. It always made me feel funny when they were around, although her dad seemed to like me. Her mom would subtly come on to me when we were alone or on the phone, and then tell Heather what a horrible mistake she was making getting involved with me. Mom sort of sabotaged the whole relationship, as Heather was bright and sort of on the intellectual side. But she was a local country girl, and her mom ran her life. She was also, tall, robust, and very enthusiastic regarding sex, love and the other thing. I often thought of her as Brooke Shields on steroids. She lettered five times in volleyball with the Pasco high school team.

I sip cold beer from the cooler in the back seat and wander back over time to when Heather first mentioned to me her fantasy of exploring erotic activities like so called group sex, and what the touch of another woman, in particular, would be like. I think all men fantasize about their girl friends bringing this up. All normal men any way. And especially older, jaded men like me. I'm also certain women do similar things.

It should be just like a man's she said, if you close your eyes and let go. Well, I'm for that. Except for the mustache, in most cases. She is driving, and I put my hand on her exposed thigh. She is wearing shorts in the warm spring weather, and her legs are spread open, warmed softly from the sun. Her shorts are really short. This is nice, because it exposes the huge expanse of her long, and very muscular legs, and makes her crotch snug up really nice in front. I like it...She turns and smiles and I slowly caress her, moving slowly along the smooth warm surface of her skin.

I trace my fingers around and gently massage from her knee to her groin, pressing at times into her, causing her to shift and moan. Heather is tall, with large, full, white freckled breasts, and she reaches into her cotton top, pulling one out into the open, exposing the hard rubbery tip of the nipple to my view. I have always found the legs and buttocks of women the most arousing, at least from an overall perspective. Now, I like it all, that's the truth. Especially if the skin is nice. Smooth skin seems critical, along with good hygiene. So anyway, Heather's breasts are large and lovely. Big, heavy, and her nipples are gigantic, with huge responsive red areolas.

I bend down and toward her, taking the large thick fleshy thing into my mouth, between my teeth, and suckling it deep into my throat. The size of her fills my mouth and throat, and I gasp for breath, timing the in and out motion, quickly exciting her, and feeling her entire body move and writhe in the bucket seat of the little car. When I disengage from her, my penis has grown, thick and hard, and presses against the light cotton fabric of my own shorts. Heather reaches over, with her long, strong fingers, and grabs it, pulling it free, and with hard, rapid strokes, she brings me to orgasm, with thick white spurts of my juice pumping into her encircled fingers. She continues pumping, until the sensitivity is too much, and I push my own hand onto hers, smearing the juices around my skin. She wipes with long smearing motions, the inside of her legs and mine with the white creamy juices, bringing a musky odor into the car, as we continue down the road toward the ocean. How can she do all this while driving the Mustang?

My legs become sticky as the stuff dries. I think about how much I love this woman, who brings me such intense joy, this wonderful creature who one day will leave me, and I will be changed forever, again. This may have been the first time I really tried everything I could think of to be good, get close, be honest, and love someone all the way...all the time. I am one who knows nothing, and continues, for no good reason, to try and try again...This really was Heather's idea. I didn't care one way or another, as long as she was with me.

So one day, while loosely planning our ocean weekend with Jim and Nikki, we discuss how we might approach this thing, since the premise was we were in love and living together and all that. She has always wanted to approach another woman for this type of encounter, but growing up in a small town, and not wanting to be branded as a deviate, or losing a good friend, she had always just sort of subdued the desire, the experience. She also felt that she would enjoy it more, be more relaxed, if the event involved a boy friend too, somebody like me, who would participate, but not feel threatened, or pose a threat himself.

We agree that between us, we will treat the entire episode as erotic play, assuming we could identify someone we felt we could trust and approach and we all live happily ever after. No hang-ups, no fuckups, no bullshit. I was in great anticipation actually. The thought of sharing a bed with two beautiful young women had played into my mind many times, and I was probably as prepared to go forward with the plan as anyone could be. Heather was stunning, six feet tall and athletic, with full thick lips and breasts, muscular thighs, rippling buttocks and the scent of glacial snow between her thighs. Fresh and sweet, there was a virginal, earthy aura about this woman. She was natural, easy going, sensual, and fearless.

The first time I asked her about anal sex, she said she had never tried it, but wasted no time getting on the edge of the bed, doggy fashion, with her bottom exposed. I wiped lotion all over her backside, and slowly pressed my hardness between her cheeks. The tight round muscle resisted slightly, but then opened easily, and I glided fully into her, the unique pressing of her anus, was tight and exciting. How easily I rocked back and forth, standing fully upright, hand on her large white hips, while she gasped in pleasure, begging for me to go harder and deeper.

"My God that feels good" she gasped, grunting with each pump of my hips into her. I do so enjoy being compared to a God. "I'm coming with you in my ass! It's so nice and big in me" she whispered hoarsely, pumping in time with me, harder and more aggressively. I felt my sex juice rise fast and hot, almost burning as they pumped through the length of my flesh and into her muscular backside. She was opening and closing against me, as she bucked and squirmed. I burst and popped out, watching the juice ooze out and down her thighs. She was so clean, and so good to me.

    I reached forward and lay across her back, both hands circling around to massage her breasts, slowly as we cocooned against one another. As we slowed in our breathing, our sticky hot crotches nestled together, gently pressing and releasing, pressing and rocking, sliding together, her wetness opening thickly and accepting the slight firmness that remained with me, drawing close, warm into her groin, causing me to grow again. We fucked for hours that afternoon, and every minute is clear in my memory, a gift from an angel, I suppose. There are angels walking the earth, but that's about it, as far as I know.

    I asked Heather about her friend Jane who owned and operated a small fruit orchard on the Yakima River with her husband. They had grown up together, were best of friends and Jane was very friendly, almost flirtatious with me, whenever we got together. No, they were too close, and went too far back. She was afraid Jane might have some sort of homophobic response that could create a permanent and lasting issue between them. Too bad, I really liked Jane. Tarzan like Jane...

    And, sadly, after some thought, there was really no woman in her inner or outer circle of friends and acquaintances that she felt would be comfortable with a social approach of this nature. Heather was twenty-three years old, and had lived most of her life in the limited social confines of the Tri-Cities region of south central Washington State. Lots of farmers and a perversely high number of scientists and engineers, all living easily on the federal government's job program at the site of the nation's early nuclear production program; a living monument to the Cold War. But I have this friend from school too.

Jim, may his hair never fall out, may his toenails never grow fungi, and his buttocks be forever firm and supple. So I call Jim and tell him that Heather has this idea about a group nude massage/orgy and we can't find any females but does he possibly know any and does he want do it anyway as in like just the three of us and pretty much anything goes? He paused for some time as I recall, and even though he was hundreds of miles away, I could see him shifting, smiling slightly, nodding his head, of course he loves the idea, I thought, who wouldn't? "Sure", he finally replied, "sounds like fun!" He thought his former girl friend might come along, but she had prior commitments.

A vision unfolds, euphoric, tumbling over limbs and flesh, flushing, drawing deep currents of midnight air, shimmering selves, dissolving in stone, eternal, inconceivable. The complementary natures emerge, naturally, through the cultural ideologies and nonsense. I dream, flesh of humans, sex of beings, hieroglyphic light patterns of blue and green rush over the shore grass. Three hearts in the ocean moon, alabaster, smooth in the cool light, floating in the moist surf air, tingling dreams of fingers, hips and bottoms, fleshy parts, moist, slippery, shimmering the deep groins and reflexes of our sex. I wonder how the first touch will come. Slowly? Or the first greeting? Thousands of images occur to me, like railroad cars in a dark carnival; red is my heart, dark as midnight the eyes that are mirrors to my soul. Somewhere over China a bird reels and floats...

The intense sun of southeast Washington radiates the air as I sit in the afternoon stillness conjuring roses, smoking the herb of paradise. So fitting that the worlds most enormous nuclear waste dump be inhumanly hot, dry, lifeless and otherworldly. Like stepping out onto the sun, I imagine. Far away and distant a ringing sound shatters the image like a child's soap bubbles, decomposing and rearranging themselves into unfamiliar forms.

Someone invisibly picks up a phone and places it near my head. Its Nikki, the other high school buddy, asking for Heather. Honey drips from the handset of the teleportation device and runs over me as the song bird sings, using her voice, her dreaming, over the wires, so intoxicating. "Heathers still at work, Nikki," I say. Eventually, she reveals she is looking for something to do over the weekend and I mention our ocean retreat. Outside the window, a little bird goes hopping and chirping...

Now we are four. She lives in Olympia, so will meet us in Long Beach. I call Jim and tell him Nikki is coming too. He tells me he hasn't had sex with anyone or anything in over two years. Really? He should kill himself then. Heather walks in and unfolds her things onto the table. Nikki wants to come along this weekend, I tell her. I enjoy the sight of her full red lips, moist and juicy, as she removes her vest and the fullness of her breasts jiggle in my eyes. Slowly pressing into her bosom, our mouths touch and explore each other like thick vaginas with penises, probing tongues and fleshy holes. Her large meaty thigh presses into my groin, the warm flesh of her chest and belly contracting and expanding. I rub her bottom with my fingers, feeling through the silky dress and running along the slit of her bottom. "Great, maybe she'll hit it off with Jim," she replies. Maybe she'll hit it off with you, I wonder...

Heather strolls through the green and blue light to the brown cedar rest stop huts, her thick hips swaying gently in the patterned dusk of the forest. She is sex reborn, in radiant hues, drawing me like a hound, lusty, natural and unquestioning, robust and astounded by my self. I feel my groin, massage the male piece of me through the soft cotton sweats, dream of stars on the ocean, follow her with my eyes from the passenger seat of the little Mustang. Dusk encircles us, greenish gray and thick, surreal as my muscles turn limp and I step from the car like a Raggedy Ann doll, loose and powerful in the oceans spell, still hours from the hotel but sensing the nearness of the coast.

Gulls make their sad wailing cry, and I am now in the eye of the bird looking down. Two human figures far below, one and apart, millions of souls are seemingly drifting and balanced in the same moment. I drop the empty beer can in the recycle bin and turn to face her. She smiles and approaches, the river is wind sweeping her long thick hair. Elven dust is gleaming in the air around Heather. With deep liquid eyes, her blood red lips thick and full, she firmly wraps around me, pulling gently in and easing fingers into my cotton pants, grasping the thickness of my bottom, pulling me up against her hips. A car rolls by quietly in living rubber and steel, oblivious to our presence. I float as she plunges her tongue down my throat, thickly, eager to open her lust. We have no words, no need for words. The pine trees perfume the evening and dusk is here and the birds are here...

"I'm excited about tonight" she gurgles through the watery atmosphere of the riverside, memories of mushrooms filling my head. "Me too" I gurgle back, from fathoms of ocean, eons of culture converging to eradicate and destroy our sense of wonder, mystery, passion, eros. How then do we come to this? Somewhat by design, somewhat by chance? We are of the ancient ones, knowledge pure and unshackled, the final resting place of Buddha, dissolving the facades, drifting in bliss, death must be wonderful, and of course Whitman is right. Here beneath my feet he rises, from the mud and grass and pine cones and squirrel droppings, consuming the physical world with fiery eyes, hidden from normal perceptions, we glow with light and energy, spiraling around the fleshy bones and meat of us, two birds circling blue and white in the darkening sky.

I press the fleshy top of her with my hands, thumbs indenting her big round nipples into the white t-shirt and eliciting a throaty groan and smile. "We should get going again, Gary. They are waiting for us by now." So we strap back into the steel machine and resume our headlong plummet over the river road. I put the window down and look up at the sky. There are always birds, and only a little bird turd...

Long Beach comes into view, it is nearly dark now, late dusk I guess, cool and windy. We are close to the oceanfront hotel, with the lovely two bedroom suite, full kitchen and pass through bar with seating for four. Driving slowly through town, the ocean front tourist town with the carnival feel, bleached wood and colorful shops full of kites and other quick sale items, the facades come alive.

Explain the ocean to me, father. Why do I feel it so, why is my heart the center of my soul? Why is my heart my mind, and my mind my consciousness? Why are words so fucking big? The sound of it, the smell, the energy and power of movement, water, these things are the ocean. Humans cannot live here for long, it is too strong for them. Adrenaline seeps into my system, hormones push the blood of my veins with more urgency, the Aikido master awakens, takes a seat near the bar, waits patiently. On the outskirts of town we leave the empty streets and continue north the two and a half miles or so to the hotel. "I'm starving" Heather remarks.

We check in, find our room, grab some stuff from the back seat and trunk, and head up the stairs to the top level. I walk in first and see Jim and Nikki come from around the corner of the hallway. They arrived several hours before us and have been getting to know each other a little. They both look great, Jim in jeans and a softly patterned casual shirt and Nikki with her spray on jeans and tank top, tight and light, stunning to behold. I gush in my heart, smiling at them both. "It's about time you two got here" Jim says, laughing like he does so easily and reaching toward me. I take his hand, we hug, pressing lightly into one another, as one entity, as true companions. Heather pushes into us and envelops Jim in her enormous body, spanking him playfully on the left cheek of his buttocks. Nikki and I embrace in turn, finding each other in the moment. For the first time I see her, pulling the supple body to me she yields fully, pressing like warm living Jell-O on my senses, scented of the deeper woods, and a little sun tan lotion. I rub her back gently, standing in the sea of flesh, drift slowly to her bottom with small circular massage strokes, opening her with a subtle tug of her bottom. She does not fear it I think, everything is good.

The two girls embrace as Jim and I finish unpacking the car. Soon we are drinking fresh cocktails and smoking hashish, laughing, brushing our bodies in open flirtations, revealing four hearts, and four souls colliding. Breathing deeply, allowing the colors in, drifting in erotic pools of blue and green, I lose my sense of self, rotate within, dissolve into light, recall years later the language forms, find ice in my glass and drink, feel eyes floating before me, move again into this human body. I drink deeply…for tomorrow we die.

Jim and I relocate out on the large deck facing the ocean dunes, leaving the girls inside. A dull constant roar surrounds us, the sky is fully dark now and star filled, laughing voices drift melodic, like wind chimes, like colliding bubbles. The ocean air is full of smells, the wind gusts and flows around us. I see the cold steel and glass of ancient lighthouses scanning the fog, crying like sea monsters over the spray and deep swells of water boiling over the horizon, distant and alone. "Nikki is beautiful" Jim illustrates, smiling and bending over the small pocket pipe I carry for smoking the buds of marijuana plants, opium when I have it. His face is aglow in orange dream light, wicked and mildly mad in his countenance. "No shit" I restate his observation, neither of us having ever seen her before. Its true, she has the wonderfully waspish figure of a standard, classic, California beach girl, liquid movements, soft face and eyes and flirtatious mannerisms. I will never forget her face, or fail to become a little sad remembering her fears...

    Jim sits and hands me the pipe, I turn and gaze over the dunes toward the sea. The moment is out of time, out of normal consciousness. The norms of culture, the taboos we learn to use to conceptualize every event are somehow meaningless. I don't think it, I feel it. Energy flows through me and I am unconscious of body and mind separation. Floating sensations and visions of unusual dimension occur, alive in a wonderful way. I become unmasked and naked. Mushrooms, mist and sea grass, slate blue grey clouds assembling mansions in the sky.

    "It will be interesting to see if she follows through" Jim remarks. I wonder also. Turning toward one of my favorite people, I see centuries of diverse universal concepts, ideas humans have expressed flowing in his eyes like billions of miniature movie reels, swirling and colliding, blending into pure fundamental colors, kaleidoscopic and singular, uniting instantaneously. I understand without knowing, conceive without thinking, drooping languages of many cultures fade like old sheets, we are traveling beyond, soaring somehow with unknowing crystalline beings.

"Well, she seemed like she was all for it over the phone" I remark. We talk about eating, decide to go down to the dunes where the hotel grills are located and fire up some steaks. The wind is slowly becoming stronger, it is still just barely cool outside, and beautiful as a tropical storm. These must be the Chinook winds that the first nation people speak of...I become drunk from this.

The fire heats up quickly in the steady breeze, and we find some shelter in the lee of the large cabana. Not another soul to be seen, the firebox glows, dancing shadows surround us. Heather moves over the grassy earth with smooth supple energy. Her long thick hair is swinging over her muscular back, as she laughs aloud, enticing us all with her raw humor and easygoing nature. Her thick breasts, so heavy and full beneath the thin sweater, are bursting and obvious in their lust. I drink her like wine, she is the wind and ocean. She is my sister, the moon.

Jim and Nikki sit talking on the picnic bench while I attend to the steaks. Heather slides into me and puts a hand down the back of my shorts, rubbing slowly and smiling with her huge liquid brown eyes. She gently uses her powerful fingers to massage the crack of my ass, opening me like sweet candy. Our pressing chests encourage our kissing tongues, while the flames of the fire crackle and hiss. The mists of the salty ocean water drip around us, fluttering like silk sheets. swooning our souls through the dark, surreal ocean night.

I yield easily to her probing and lower the front of my pants down to reveal my self. It is hanging there so large and obvious, and she warms it and softly strokes the swollen purple testicles. Ten thousand years ago I awaken to the dawn, crying over the red hills. Brother Wolf, how long I have missed you...my travels will soon be over. Go to the eagles and the four corners, and speak to them. Bodidharma will soon return to his home...make everything ready.

There is a sweet smell of corn and beef searing on the fire. The slow rhythm of Heather's long fingers stroking my thickness, the sight of Jim and Nikki over by the tall grass, bundled in smoke and myst frames my consciousness in a singular moment. I lean my head back, as ice cold beer rushes down me...as my spirit cry fills the sky, the sea, the earth and the moon.

Heathers zippered shorts fall down and I touch her thick fleshy vaginal folds, wet and inviting as my fingers slip in one at a time. Her knees buckle and shake as she presses her pubis against my hand. My penis is hard and oozing as I rub it against her belly, smearing the slippery fluid over her warm skin, tracing the dark brown line of pubic hair that reaches into her panties. She continues gently stroking me as we stand in the fire light under the big cabana. "I think the steaks are ready" hisses from my lungs in breathy absurdity, a foolish stage whisper. Who are we hiding from? "Perfect timing" she says. I flop the large swelling of me back into the waist band of my sweat pants while she wriggles back into her shorts, pulling the zipper up with a grunt. I am no longer able to think in my first language, or any language for that matter. Four universes are colliding in this place, and the meaning is the touch of our bodies. Never before, has it been like this. The blending of consciousness, the integration of souls, the meaning of zero, and I was there, in one long, instantaneous weekend, that went on forever...To this very day, and I thank you all my companions, I continue to shine...

    Heather and Nikki pull the cobs of corn off the fire grill and Jim takes up the meat. I sip on my drink and follow the three of them back across the sandy lawn to our suite. On the way we are passed by other humans, grinning foolishly and speaking ridiculous tomes of greeting in one of the common tongues of the middle range people. They are quickly frightened off by the North Dwellers and seamlessly absorbed by the darkness and stars. Up the stairs and in, we manage to consume the food and restore some order to the large kitchen. Dark is now all around us, occasional stars shining through the high overcast ocean sky. The mist shrouds the whole scene in a twilight surrealism. No moon though, not tonight. Jim sets and lights a fire in the large stone fireplace, the eerie light providing psychedelic shadows and caricatures of the open living room and lounge. Conversation is slowed and less frequent, more subdued and relaxed it seems, human forms sensing and responding to the delicate moves of our bodies, subtle and inviting, giving and yielding. There is an elephant in the room.

    Bubbles form in my mouth, quietly bursting in the middle of the room. Who would like a massage? Someone whispers distractedly, shattering souls and self images in a single pure tone. Nikki shimmers in her seat, rotating her head like a lighthouse at sea. Here is the Cheshire cat, revealing and mysterious, flexing its claws and neck, purring inviting, drawing us in and caressing our bowels. Yes, she will be happy to lie down for us all, undress and yield to loving fingers. Heather wants to rest and moves to the private bedroom to rest, kissing my mouth deeply before Jim and I open the large foldout bed in front of the fire. The movement begins.

Now we are sailing over the ocean, we are like ships at sea ,beckoning and returning signals of hope and encouragement. This is the moment of wonder and discovery, enchanted evening of dreams, where children never grow old and there is no pain or sorrow. All souls are open and loving, and there is no deceit, no ulterior design. A third eye is following her into the darkened bedroom, following within and without, becoming her lust and passion, accepting with abandon the pushing thrusts of me into her seething flesh. Our merging souls reflect harmonious and full, like alpine lakes in a summer day. She pulls the flesh of me open and consumes my gaping soul, like dolphins rushing home for Christmas. So that's it.

The fire glows cool and red now, popping and sizzling with steam and pitch. Candles flicker near the open deck and around the head of the foldout hotel bed with the warm flannel sheets. Nikki stands staring out the window toward the sea or something, fingering her wine glass with casual indifference. Nikki, I muse aloud, why don't you lie down and take off your clothes? We can start with you doing some group massage...

Jim and I look at each other through the smoky night...we understand there are no barriers. Not really. So she says nothing and reaches down to her beltline with both hands, pulling her sweater off in one smooth motion. She is a dancer, I think. Moving like trees when the wind blows, like an Indian spirit, like a ghost, like a lover, like the mountain. Turning from the ocean she tosses the flimsy cashmere toward her sleeping bag against the far window and grasps the belt buckle of her jeans. Her eyes become purple and blue universes, dying and evolving galaxies, quieting and containing the force of her, penetrating Jim and me like dogs of Beelzebub.

Stepping forward and out of the cotton blue jeans, Nikki trips on to the warm sheets of the bed, turning instantly copper in the angled light of the fireplace. She rolls immediately onto her back. Her belly is smooth and sweet like new fruit. I radiate from within, Jim swoons and moans. Slowly, and as Siamese twins, we approach from opposite sides of her. Nikki stretches and spreads her self over the surface of the thin sheets, her now opened body scented like jungle herbs and spices. She is caressing herself with our eyes, flexing her tiny, supple hips up and forward, then revolving over on to her stomach. Her bottom is pear shaped and fleshy. Small and blonde, her cleavage forms a lovely triangle of creases into her bottom. She is sweetened and moist with natural oils or something. I think of ripe fruit for the first time this night. Jim and I look through each others eyes and smile hilariously, the beauty and wonder of this enrapturing our sensibility, giddy on the wind.

 I press next to Nikki's chest with my folded leg and rest my hand on her upper back, rotating and soothing her with my touch and thoughts, slowly and with large circular motions. My eyes close and my head rolls back. With both hands now I make large strong circular motions over the slender muscles of her back and neck. Jim is manipulating at her feet and she breathes deeply as she groans and sighs, as if she was having a slow, continuous orgasm. I work on her face and neck muscles while admiring the nudity of her body spread before me on the sheets, and of Jim happily rubbing oil and fingers into her legs and thighs.

 I feel a light tapping on my shoulder, and turn to find Heather sitting on the floor beside me. She is wearing a purple, lavender silky under piece called a Teddy, I think. It is short on top, with bikini panties below, and she smells like she bathed in a cloud of spring wild flowers. She smiles and drops her eyes, sort of in a bashful way, and begins rubbing and pulling at my leg. Nikki says she is getting sleepy, and so Heather, Jim and I decide to move into the master bedroom, and let her get some rest out by the deck.

Heather's hair hangs to her waist, and the swaying that it makes as she leads the way through the suite and the halls is absolutely enchanting. Ask me, and I will describe every detail of it for you. I paint her, this first day, and over and over again, from every conceivable angle, as she flowers in my mind. I am falling into the sun, and I am back with her, from the first day I saw her, until she told me to go. I follow my tears from that river, and expose my soul in the dry dust of the central desert. I curl up alone in cool flannel sheets, and I feel my only one, close behind me, next to me, rolling me over onto my stomach. I am pinned now, until she finishes her roaming, her probing, and we embark in clouds and dreams, to the far mountains, and the blue, blue oceans...

In the back master bed, she sprawls and opens, like a condor on the full bed. The fullness of her is accentuated and amplified somehow, as Jim and I come to her from opposite sides of the bed. She laughs and giggles as we tease her, and goes back and forth in the most natural way I have ever seen. For the rest of the night, we rock and tumble, and rest and caress each other. This angel, this dream of feminism and modernity, takes these two old men in rapture and joy indescribable. On and on we go, until we all fall asleep, together, in a bundle, in exhaustion and perfection. This, the most incredibly erotic time of my life. In the morning, Jim brings in coffee and sweet rolls, while we all three of us languish in the bed smoking and drinking and eating. Nikki sleeps alone on the deck, and the world is puddle wonderful, and the universe is ocean blue, forest green, and the sky goes on forever. Somewhere over China, a bird reels and floats.

Once up and showered, we all go to town for lunch and some cold beer. Then, we scurry back to the lodge and the next night is a cool repeat of the night before. Nikki kept pretty much to her self, unfortunately. I felt odd and somehow sad about this, as she seemed so enthusiastic during our planning discussions. I felt she was missing out somehow, that she desired to engage with us, but some fear kept her back.

There were no surprises or concealments in this party, as we all felt an open forum would lead to the greatest success for all, in terms of enjoying the outing and doing something deeply erotic, for at least one time in the lives of each of us. It pretty much worked out, I think, even though Nikki sort of drifted off alone as the intimacy and erotic moments deepened, so to speak. I think the mutual respect we all felt, and the openness and honesty, allowed the time to go well for all four of us.

To you all, Namaste! I hope some day, as you read this characterization of the days, you will think well of me, and the time we shared. And, just so you understand me quite clearly, I am ready for an encore any time...

Can you ever go back in time?
Don't ask me!
What is time, again?
I thought time was money?

before dawn

You are the floating moon,
Over the blue lake,
Of the green heart,
Shimmering brilliantly in the stillness of me.

waking

My heart went running to the sea,
My eyes flow to the ocean.
I saw the stars surrounding thee,
Where the owl and dog had spoken.

Dreaming

So it is and shall forever be.
Dreamland is no simple journey.
And when you come, dearest darling,
Wear your darkest black robes, bring your cream whitest
    skin.
Bring your blood red lips child, and the winds of Persia
    wrapped in blue and green silk.
We will open them.
The rest will follow.

Twilight

My darling young one,
I am unable to compare my self to these charmers you
    speak of,
Since I do not mix with them.
Are they like the Fakirs of India, who trick the eyes and
    minds of the herd with levitation robes and other
    illusory devices?
You create this poetry in me,
I simply form the words and images.
I am, that is all.

Lynette

Hi! It's me, Gary Jones, a ghost from the summer of 1979, if my memory serves me correctly. Have twenty five years really gone by so quickly? I am sure you must remember me, Bob Toombs, and Fred Aldrich? The Ballard Boys, as we used to call ourselves. Are you still friends with Patty? I so hope this letter reaches you somehow and that all is well with you and yours. I drove by your house today on Brown's Point, and noticed that the mailbox still has the family name on it. So here I am writing this note, hoping beyond hope that your family is still connected with this address and that I will be able to contact you.

Not a day of my life goes by that I regret losing you, so many years ago. There is so much I would like to explain. What I remember so wonderfully is the beauty that was you, the soft, loving, compassionate, mysterious you. Please write to me, if your life circumstances allow. I am living alone now, have for many years, and have two grown children. Oh, and a granddaughter named Emily. She is two years old. I am living in Tacoma again following a 2 year hermitage on the Quinault River, and plan to settle here for the remainder of my life, and live quietly on my boat or in a small house, to write and enjoy the simple wonder and beauty of this world.

I love you Lynette. I loved you when we met, and was a fool to have treated you like I did when I went into the Air Force. Please forgive me, and give me one more chance. I know I am making a lot of assumptions here, and being quite bold with my propositions. But, I figure I have nothing to lose, and the world to gain. You may be married and happily free to ignore me, forget me, or whatever. I pray this is not the case, and we can at least have lunch together sometime. Maybe at the Cliff House like we used to do.

Take care, and I will understand if I never hear from you. I am writing a book, and have entered a new profession as a massage therapist, after 20 years of technology and corporate type stuff, I am going back in time to my hippy heart and soul, where I belong, and playing my guitar again, and writing poetry about the beautiful things in life. I drive a Honda Element, the environmental car from Honda, and have a grown puppy named Bodi, a long haired American Dingo. I spend most of my time at the beach, and in the parks of the area, wherever there is water and blue, blue skies. I have always sought the natural and still places of the planet.

Please call or write. I love you Lynette. You still live in my heart and soul like yesterday never went, like time never existed. I still feel the warmth of your hand squeezing mine in the cool of the night. Do you still like to hold hands when you take walks with a friend? Namaste...gj

Message for Lynette

Then I think we should make plans together on a regular, permanent, full time basis, until the end of time...can you handle that? Can we do it in a most gentle and loving way for all concerned? Can we make the most of the becoming of us all? May I adore thee and all you love for all the greatness they conceal within? Love me, and I will love you in return, as we are both gods, and capable of anything...of this I am certain...gj

Sand

Firmly I stand, feet rooted in the earth.
The muddy gravel of this creek bed shifts slightly as I turn this way and that.
Far off the horizon stretches with yellow and green grasses,
They are swaying violet,
As the suns rays make the scene a kaleidoscopic storm of color,
Pastels and pinks, corals and blue,
Blue, blue skies puffing gargantuan clouds over all,
They diminish the tiny figures and life forms into the slightest, smallest grains of sand.
We came to watch, to walk and fly,
We came to stretch that thing of us that must go moving forward,
That which lifts each bird of the coast into the rising currents of airborne particles, Invisible but sustaining,
Rising with natural ease toward the warming suns and planets.
They circle every where in time and space, you know
They are dumbly blinking.
I sense my own body, clumsy and awkward, out of place,
Just as natural am I, as evolution slowly forms us throughout the eons
We become what we are.
No story can explain me, nor sign show me the way.
No song can herald my coming.
I was never here,
I was the null, and I was the void,

Now I am all, all that is.
Beyond the moist drip of my eye,
To all I survey, all that I comprehend with patterned words,
All this is foreign.
Here, I reach my fingers into my coat, grasp the cool glass bottle I find there,
Placing it to my lips, I drink, drink soundly and fully.
The cold liquid essence soothes my throat, enters my body, my blood,
Opening me slowly and delightfully with rushes of color and wind.
The wind is my brother, and moves around me like some Aladdin's carpet,
So then I become borne away to distant places, lands of magical beings,
Perhaps to where the giant ones dwell, the elves of the machine.

Where there is beauty, mystery, joy, woven into the essential fabric,
This is each moment of existence.
Never forgotten, my brother, my sister, my lover and companion,
And you, yes you too! Who follow me with quiet breathing.
Too close we have come again, with too little caution.
Are there others watching?
We must use extreme care, that this place should remain for us, unspoiled, for we know they would make it thus.
They would trample and degrade this one place.

Yes, I know how they would also deliberately and maliciously destroy the rarest children we have raised, the radiant ones.

Come sit behind these eyes with me, for a while, I can
    protect and conceal you.
I kiss you upon your sweet lips,
The distant perfume of the first ever rose fills my
    consciousness, my nostrils,
I cry for the lost wonders of the earth,
The dream of the beast approaches.

Ghost Riders

On the snowy river under a winter's night, I sent a druid fire to the sky and the moon was soft as the snow came down all around me.

In this fire went all the things I thought were connections from you, like letters and notes and cards and vouchers for songs you make with money.

In this smoke were visions, promises, dreams and the like, and they floated perfectly into nothing, into the stars and the deepening sky.

How clear and sad the mad stillness is and how insane the last moment of you will sit with me forever.

My sadness grows for you in your terror and your pain, and the horrid vision of a twisted sister who screams at you in her derangement.

A brutal vision of what destroyed the spirit, heart and love of you. I saw in horror one of the dark sources of what made you.

Who cries for the lone wolf who sees through the cold night, who comes to comfort you in your palace of shadows?

Who comes picking buttercups, to place gently upon your eyes, that you may sleep and dream in peace, knowing simply you are loved for the sake of love?

Who breathes each breath with the soul of you, that you are one with the other, and there is no story beyond or more beautiful?

Whose fingers move over you and say speak no more of the world outside, you are for my body and I am for your body?

Turn back, for a single moment, there is something following you just beyond reason, beyond reach, beyond recovery.

No, please forgive me, there is nothing. It is the wind. It is the earth. It is the river. It is the dark, eyeless beast, who comes no more...

Mon Sheri, how did we miss each other?

Were we once upon a time a pair,
A knowing, foolish couple, who met and lived,
And wondered and loved and failed and missed and struck with certainty the center of it? Am I in this place now so far down stream of time and space,
So removed from what we knew, what we were, and all it was in our hands to keep?
Did we look so hard to find each other
That we saw clear through what was nakedly present, blatantly obvious?
Did the fire cover the hearth, with such intensity,
That we could not be still in the comfort and warmth of our house?
Did we rise as the Phoenix, and consume ourselves in fire and ash?
I had you, I know this.
I still live in these moments where I can sense it.
It is clear like some wizard's crystal, hovering in my third eye,
The eye that is my mind, my conscious stream of images of all I perceive.
This I know in my most deep soul of souls,
That we are one, that we were one,
And this moment that was, had it's time then,
But is also a living moment in me now, and that this moment also lives in you.
Here is the hint at the timelessness of all things, and the concept of the eternal.

Here is proof of the human and nonhuman soul.
The soul of souls cannot be denied.

And you know it as well, for we were two,
Long fooled and searching, ignoring the close in things,
The subtle, charming turn of a wrist, to hold your hand,
To close over you in the pocket of my large coat and warm you.
To turn and kiss you with no warning
And the moon is my answer to the unspoken question in your eyes.
You who loved me, who took me away from all earthly and empty moments,
And so pure was the way of us, the full warmth of your face and lips,
Turned slightly toward me on the stormy bridge over the Ballard fishing terminal.
In my arms I held the complete story of time, in you,
And the touch of my hips to yours, and this is where we end it.
With the terrible sense of my only loving child,
Whose grasp on my fingers is slowly worn to exhaustion by the pull of the storm,
The flood and waters of the great storm that rise about us
And all I can do is for naught!
I can no longer sustain or compete!

We are lost, my loving one, this only I know for certain.
So in this timeless moment I die, and the death of me lives forever.
This is where you fade and go
And this is where the men of science sing from the steel tower
Overnight, you are gone.
And I fade into the abyss,

Weightless and buoyant like some astronaut untethered
    from his ship,
I shimmer in the moist night air,
Ghostly and pale, transcendent in my horror and my joy!
I stand on the bridge and look back at your window from
    the Ballard side.
This sudden brilliance that was you,
I still see roaring silently across the summer sky,
Hung suspended in fire and ice,
Gone forever in a moment,
Lost forever in a dream,
Mine forever in still memories,
In the forever dream that is my eternal waking mind...

For Lynette

Whose eyes are so beautiful and deep, I dream whether I
    am awake or asleep...
Where is the little boy-girl I knew?
I saw them last night by the light of the moon,
Twirling and dancing and spinning around,
The stars were all rainbows floating down.
Purple red green violet yellow and pink,
My eye said to me in the middle of a wink,
I am in a dream, I wonder I think,
My eye says "I see you" then closed with a wink!

The Mercer Island Tunnel and The House on Phinney Ridge

I do not recall your name,
I do clearly remember your face,
Your body, and the way it clung to me
One night in the basement of the old house,
The cool basement in Phinney Ridge,
This and all that accompanies it will always be fresh in
    my mind.

I know that you were with Ralph, who shared this
    house.
And you were with Bob, who also shared this house.
I know that you came often to the bar in North Seattle
    called the Aquarius,
This is where Ralph, Bob and I worked for a while,
Until Ralph lost his hand in the printing press where he
    worked days,
And Bob went back to St. Joseph Missouri where he has
    family.
And that you were so young.
And when we kissed, and you were so eager around my
    body,
That you made me love you in the wordless moment that
    I had you,
And you had me.
And perhaps most clearly I remember the fiery ride on
    my motorcycle.
It took us over the midnight lake, and the moon was so
    full it smelled

Of camp fires and moon dust.
And the throttle burned,

And we shook in the wind, and you held on to me so tight.
You held me so tight, I knew you could not let go.
No matter what, you were hanging on to me like you were part of me.
The tunnel swept us in like a vortex,
The shine of the lights,
The reflection of the brilliant tiles lining the inside tunnel walls
Flashed by like lightning and more.
And the roaring fade of the engine behind us as we leaned into the curves,
First this way, and then that way.
The front tire flutters and we seem almost airborne.
And the burst as we emerge from the tunnel,
Back under the moonlit sky.
I am rushing, and you are rushing with me, for we are not alone,
We are one together, vanishing like a comet out of the concrete tube.

There, you point, there is your house.
And I let you off the bike, and you walk home,
Up the short gravel driveway,
Goodbye, and thanks for the ride.
I open a cold beer, and drive back to the house,
The house on Phinney Ridge.
Is it Debbie?

The Virgin Meets Albert Hoffmann

Wouldn't this be easier if you took your clothes off?
I mutter some stupid thing, and do as I am told.
She catapults on top of me, and presses her fingers into my face.
And I feel something soft and furry moving over my stomach and groin,
An odd but very nice sensation.
This is close, I think, this is doing it.
She is getting more and more physical.
Cherie had taken two double purple barrels of so called Owsley,
Lysergic acid diethylamide-25 or LSD.
It was a special concoction for the Monterey Blues Festival circa 1968.
It was distributed freely by some eccentric millionaire,
Who got it straight from Albert Hoffman at Sandoz pharmaceutical labs in Switzerland.
The bread and butter days of the summer of love...
Keep it alive, keep it alive...
Cough, hack, drool...
We were very well connected teenagers in the west and north ends of Tacoma.
My friend Terri had a car, a Buick Roadmaster, I think, with a three speed,
A three speed on the column, that is.
We filled it with bulk oil and siphoned gas every Friday night.
And we drove to the University District in Seattle.

Fortieth and University Way, I think it was.
The local hippies ran an open air market for every drug you could imagine.
And the shit was cheap.
And, surprisingly, it was good.
We netted enough on our allowances,
Combined with Terri's job at Central Meats where he worked with his dad as a butcher, To buy anything we wanted.

We would in turn share it with friends from school for a small profit.
We stuck pretty much to the psychedelics and marijuana.
Eventually, we hit a regular, trusted connection.
He was a chubby little faggot from North Seattle who worked at Boeing.
His name was Scott.
I think Terri was engaging in fellatio with Scott.
So it goes.
I could not pronounce fellatio at this time,
And besides, did I mention Terri had a car?
Scott flew to San Francisco about once a week.
He came back with a couple of suitcases full of dope, mostly pot and acid.
Owsley was giving LSD out for free. He was some millionaire genius.
He made the Monterey batch.
Cherie was getting really high and horny.
I know this now.
It has all been explained to me now by those who know.

By those who knew.
I had no idea how to engage in sex with anything but an athletic supporter,
And a locked bathroom door.

Cherie did. She knew how, that is.
She squirmed and wiggled around on top of me until my little virgin penis was so hard I thought the skin was going to burst.
And then, and then!
Yes! She was on top, and she was wet and slipping around and then she did it!
She sat on my fat, engorged glans and sat down hard! And she kept on going.
She pumped me like a dog, and somehow, I ended up on top of her,
And the most incredible feeling shook my entire being.
I came inside of her and it was the most exquisite feeling I had ever experienced.
I have since learned to try and stay on the bottom...

This is why we live, my friends, dear people.
This is the meaning of existence.
When sex and orgasm end, you are as the dead rotted tombs of Egypt.
I am nothing. I am the waste that blows over the highest mountains.
I thank you now, my young friend.
You taught me so much, and you were so beautiful.
I am sorry your parents put you in a cage.
I hope you made it out and through with minimal damage.
I make this observation, and it is no exaggeration.
Cheri was perfect.
Dark, with creamy white skin, firm breasts, and full lips.
The young Elizabeth Taylor, but more intriguing and sexual.
Intercourse.
Take me back there.

I am all for it.
My tongue is for your tongue and what is sex consumes
 me.
Especially when she is fourteen.
And when I am fifteen.
Sweet dreams of you, so real and so true.
I have no intention of pressing charges.
Although, I suppose you could say, she was my teacher.
Dear Cheri...Namaste, All my stars for thee.
These are the best of times.
We should, as a culture, encourage it.
Responsible, intimacy.
Huxley probably covered it best in his novel, Island.
Say this again...Responsible intimacy.
Sanctioned loving between humans will prevent diseases
 and pregnancies.
The moralists have fucked up local communities beyond
 recognition.
I learned about physical love at the age of 15.
And I am still at it, every chance I get.
I have found no improvement.
I will even forego alcohol for this activity.
Whew! Imagine that...

The Matsen Farms

As a young boy, I would spend at least part of every
    summer vacation with my friends on their farm.
The first farm was in Yelm, a small rural community
    between Tacoma and Mount Rainier.
The family had three sons, pretty close in age,
And the youngest was my age almost to the day.
Mike still believes we shared a crib at the hospital.
And he hates when his name is miscued as "Matsen."
Later in life he became prone to nervous breakdowns
And living in converted garages.
His parents moved to Alaska about the time we were
    started Junior High School
And we sort of lost touch.
Mike came to look me up after high school.
I was living off my unemployment insurance in a small
    apartment in downtown Tacoma, He was recently
    married to a voluptuous and very bright young
    woman named Suzie. They both knocked on my
    door one summer afternoon,
Right out of the blue.
I came to the door in my boxer shorts and opened it.
I am not sure I recognized either one of them,
As he had grown taller, and she was in fact a complete
    stranger.
Mike shrieked something about me exposing my self to
    his wife,
Whom he then introduced with great pride
And a lot of explanations about their life together in
    Alaska.
Mike had received some sort of Junior Achiever award

For helping people during the great and mighty earthquake of 1965.
I think it was 1965, anyway...
It was in all the papers, and sometimes they talk about it on NOVA.
Eventually, we all found ourselves living in the same city, Seattle.
They were pursuing professional degrees
In health care or dentistry, or something,
And I was taking classes for the sake of knowledge and enlightenment.
I discovered later that Suzie didn't think much of dentists,
And that Mike was slowly driving her mad
By insisting she follow his career dreams.
Mike was sucking her soul out, slowly, an ounce at a time.
Probably because she was one of those people who scores at the top of her class in everything,
Due to some sort of photographic memory or other quirk of genius that is beyond my experience.
I liked Suzie. I still like her, I suppose, if by some miracle I ever would see her again.
She was natural and sweet, and had the deepest red hair and freckles I had ever seen.
Her hair was down to her waist, and beautiful.

One Friday night I came home from work at the pharmacy about midnight,
I found a note pinned to my door.
I was helping them manage several rental properties in the area
I painted, cleaned, and that sort of stuff.
I actually bounced a tenants head one Saturday night for being noisy.
I got a free apartment, occasionally some gas money,

And the chance to work up close with Suzie.
When she paints, she wears a flimsy cotton tank top,
And those high cut shorts that don't quite cover one's bottom.
And, of course, they were hip huggers.
I enjoyed these times very much,
As Suzie would frequently come over to me and wash little drips of paint off my face,
Or legs or back with a damp cloth she kept in her hand.
She kept it so she could wipe up little drips of paint as she worked.
She was very meticulous and precise.
Suzie has the figure of a classic Vogue model,
Tall, slender, large breasted, long legs and full, pouting red lips.
I could not take my eyes off of her.
Even when she was not there.

Okay. So I take the note down, go inside and close the door behind me,
I take out an ice cold beer from the cooler in my kitchen.
It is frosty and slushy as I pour it down my throat.
The fridge is primarily to keep beer cold.
The note reads something like this:
Gary, I know you are probably tired and all that, but if you feel like it, why don't you come over for some wine tonight when you get home, if you want, that is? I am here alone watching television by my self, and would love some company. Mike is gone scuba diving with a bunch of his dive buddies in the San Juan islands. He won't be back until Sunday night or Monday...You know how he is...Just come on in, the door is unlocked! Bring some marijuana if you have any! Suzie
Sometimes the obvious is not always so clear to some of us.

Sometimes what you dream formulates slowly before you in three dimensions as you watch in amazement.
Sometimes the magic works, some times it doesn't.
I think Old Lodge Skins said something like that.
This my friends, is one of those moments, and I am not to miss it.
I took a quick shower, grabbed a small bag of my home grown shake,
And made my way like a ghost along the catwalks of the high apartment complex
We lived on the north side of Queen Anne hill.
Outside the upper story corner unit where Suzie and Mike lived, I paused.
I listened quietly at the door for signs, any signs that would tell me anything.
Then I tried looking through the peep hole, but everything seemed really far away.
I could make out lights in the kitchen, I think.
There was no sign of Mike's truck, so I took the door knob in hand and slowly twisted it. I pushed, and I was inside.
Suzie called to me from the master bedroom, further down at the end of the hallway.
My heart is pounding, and my knees are weak, a little shaky too...
I see the flickering light of candles, and walk through the bedroom doorway.
Suzie is sprawled on a large pile of pillows at the left edge of the bed,
She is wearing her familiar pink tank top and raggedy cutoff shorts.
One knee is pulled high up against her chest,
I realize she is as flexible as rubber.
Her face is flush pink and she holds a large tulip glass in her hand,
Half cocked over and ready to spill onto the bed.

A large magnum of white wine sits on the table beside her,
She says "Hello, Gary."
I say something debonair and clever in return,
I move to sit at the foot of the bed.
She invites me to come closer and asks me if I would like some wine.
I am still holding the long necked bottle of beer, but I accept anyway.
While she is in the kitchen, I fix up a marijuana cigarette, and light it.

She returns with two full glasses, and sits again at the head of the bed.
I move closer this time, and sit sort of between her legs,
They are both spread wide and long, like ocean buoys,
Suzie is directing me to home port or safe haven.
I am just a poor boy, seeking shelter from the storm.
After a few minutes of small talk, I put down my wine and roll over onto my stomach. The marijuana cigarette has long since been extinguished
It is festering along side us in a little crystal ash tray.
Suzie's brilliant red hair is everywhere,
It is luminescent in the candle light, and floating on her breast and stomach.
I bury my face in her belly button, and begin caressing her with my tongue and beard. She giggles, and squirms, and starts bucking vigorously against me.
I am a little surprised at how violently she squirms under me,
But she is laughing and holding me firmly the whole time.
I pull at her shorts, and they practically disintegrate in my fingers.

These pants were designed to crumble, perfectly at just this moment, I think.
Suzie laughs, and discards the final shreds and remnants,
She tosses them casually at the floor beside her.
Flinging my body forward like Tarzan,
I lunge at her vagina with my mouth.
She shrieks, and jumps away, bouncing on the bed like a child's toy.
Like a possessed child's toy.
She hops into the air, practically in a full back flip, and pushes me over with a grunt.
"I like you to be rough with me, you know" she grins at me.
"You mean, you want me to beat you up?" I say with some surprise.
"Yes, hit me Gary...it really excites me" she gasped.
"But I could hurt you Suzie.
I am much stronger than you, and you know I am a trained martial artist."
She said "I know. I don't want you to kill me, or break anything.
Just make it sting, and wrestle me around."
All righty then...I must confess, I feel a little out of place.
In all my days, I had not associated pain with sexual pleasure.
But, I am still practically a virgin.
So do what you are told.
Doesn't this classify as sadism, or masochism,
Or one of those other western medical diagnoses that our culture has established as taboo?
So now the young poet gets to gently beat up this vision of classic beauty,
In a real way, while we both gallop around her king sized water bed,

While we are screaming like banshees,
While we climax, we orgasm, and the juices of sex flow
       anyway,
All around us, and all over us.
And she loves me for it.

Afterwards, I return to my apartment and watch sign
       off.
I also watch the stars over the moon
I watch the lights of the Ballard Bridge and Fisherman's
       Terminal.
I am standing on my deck, and my heart returns the
       outer regions,
To outer and inner space that is my home.
I suck the smoke from a Camel filter into my lungs,
I am tasting Suzie and the lingering grape flavors of
       German Riesling in my mouth.
She is wonderful, and this night was frightening, scary
       and delightful.
They are a curious species, limitless yet constrained,
The midnight fog rolls up the hillsides of Ballard and
       Phinney Ridge,
And I am Sherlock Holmes, wandering in the streets of
       London,
Lost in my pipes and needles.
I think of Mike,
With his large diver's knife and eyes bulging out from
       behind his face mask,
Prying living Abalone from their rocky perches on the
       bottom of Puget Sound.
I hear the silence of the Abalone, bubbling out to sea.
He once asked me if my girl friend and I would like to
       have foursome.
I probably would have, but Vicki was not so excited
       about the idea.
So we never did.

I saw Suzie a number of times after this,
Before life circumstances took us away on divergent
	paths
Before she and Mike got divorced, and he went on to his
	next woman,
And she returned to Alaska.
Oddly, or so it seemed odd to me,
She never wanted to arrange time for us to be together
	alone again.
Not like a date,
Or like mature adults who are developing an intimate
	relationship and friendship.
Here is what Suzie wanted,
And this is how Suzie found her enjoyment with men.
She wants me to come find her. Not in the light of day,
When she is illuminated and lucid.
But when she is alone along a dark walkway, or in the
	alleys of Seattle,
Where dark, unknown men can take her, and push her
	down,
And press their groins into her face.
I like being raped, she once told me.
And it has to be a real rape.
Beat me, slap me, force me down in the gravel, and I will
	yield then to you,
I will open this flower of me, and you may drink my
	juices, my nectar,
And then you will go. We will not meet again.
Many years later I made efforts to contact both of my
	friends.
I found Mike through his oldest brother,
An engineer who still lived in the same house he had for
	many years,

And through his parents, who let Mike stay in their
 garage after his divorce with Suzie. She took it all,
 Mike told me.
All the money he had worked so hard to acquire over the
 years,
Everything, his properties too.
He had a nervous breakdown, and was now dating a
 pretty Japanese woman,
Last I heard, through the grapevine,
Mike met another woman and lives on her farm in
 Eastern Washington.
I wish I could see you both again, and go canoeing on
 Lake Washington.
I would like to sit in the hot sun with you, and feel the
 cool wind swirling over me.
I wish I could just be with my dear friends again,
As I remember you, in the laughing way.
Mike's last name is not really Matsen. He hates it when
 people call him Mike Matsen.
Go figure...

Brother Wolf

My brother I see you.
I see you far across the grassy field, your yellow eyes staring intently.
I see you tracking me, watching every slight movement of my body.
You wait ever so patiently, complete and settled on your haunches.
I sense deep within the subtle urging of you, for me to come back now.
Come back from where you are now with the white eyes.
Ride with me on the gentle wing of my sister the wind.
For you know she is your sister too.
Disappear like a whisper with me into the dark edge of the forest.
The bright sun of this summer afternoon reveals too much.

Our ways are hidden, subtle and intangible.
No one can follow, if we so wish it.
In the instant that our feet move forward together,
Our sister the wind bears us up and away.
High into the cool blue atmosphere we soar upon each others thoughts.
Looking down as one, upon the coiling snake.
The snake is a river, a river of thought in the hot sand below.
On into the afternoon we soar, higher and higher in the endless skies.
And deep in your eyes, deep in the hypnotic and persistent gaze that follows me,

I know your concern.
I know that you fear for me in the strange world of the
   white ghost.
Your prelinguistic telepathy sears into my
   consciousness.
I become drawn into your staring eyes,
And I fall headlong as the stars that fall from the night
   air around us.
Suddenly this false form, this human skin, dissolves
   around me.
I am your spirit kindred, and in my thoughts of you,
In this dream time where we have lived and died over
   and over since the creation time,
And we are the stars themselves.
These unfathomable pools of light that we become,
This is the real stuff of who we are.
I sit on this hard bench and stare back at you.
Am I this cloth that shrouds me?
Am I this coinage that wears holes in my pockets?
Am I the sweat that emerges on my neck,
When I am not headlong with the wind, our sister?

Spirit brother, spirit guardian,
I raced to be with you.
I raced over the snuffling earth, my feet lightly touching
   the ground,
For an instant only, because in the speed of our race we
   turn as one to flight.
Soaring, like eagles, we careen and spin.
We delight in the distinct scents of the air,
Each particle entering our beings like the mountain
   rains down into the valleys.
Side by side, on the edge of the small clearing,
I sit and stare intently at the odd manners of these
   humans.
And I am wary, for they are small and weak,

And although we bear them nothing but good fortune,
We must remain still,
Quiet and shapeless in the purple light colors of the forests edge.
We are watching, for subtle changes in the landscape.
I see the grand creations.
I see the river that is dry now,
It no longer reaches the sea.
The humans have devoured the water that runs its way along great canyons.
Millions of eons transpire.
Tribes of people and animals come and go.
Their clay huts crumble and disappear under the eyes of the sun and moon.
Where the coyote brother once ran free and unencumbered,
Iron machines now rust and glow in the dark.
The three eyed fish paddles stupidly in the marsh,
Into the mouths of mutant rodents and cats.
Somewhere over China, a bird reels and floats.

Brenda, Sister Moon

Long you have been my lover,
Long I have waited to complete you,
And be completed by you.
When you came to me at the lodge,
My heart stopped my voice from speaking.
I knew it was you,
As the dreams are so intense,
So persistent,
And so full of your power.
I knew it was finally for you to teach me.
All that had come before, or would ever come again,
You held in your strong brown hand before me.
The blue silk dress flows around you like the waters of
    the Quinault.
And just as you had stolen my voice,
I knew that my thoughts would reach you,
As in dreams, I could not see you with the words I know.
It was new, freshly risen, like the mushrooms from the
    forest floor.
And when I touched you I was lost,
I was the child at the waters edge,
And you were far greater than I.
I was nothing to you.
This I know.
You are immense and final, the power that cannot be
    seen, but is felt everywhere,
In all things.
You, Sister Wind. My greatest lover, I see you now, going
    about your business.
You move the ocean that lies before me.

You are the rain that covers the earth.
Your presence in the world is so great,
I am nothing when you pass.
When you lift me to fly with you, then I am transformed,
As our brother the wolf is transformed and born again
 within you.
In this way we come around upon ourselves, never to
 speak again.
Never to speak again in the yellow glow of his eyes...

Eyes before us, we are forever travelers in the snowy
 mountains.
The trails race by under our feet and the dark green
 trees conceal
Thoughts, dreams and wonder.
Paddling ahead, footsteps thumping softly under our
 bellies,
We run.
And we run, and we continue to run.
There is something to escape, and something to pursue.
And there is nothing to explain any of it.

And then one day, there was no where to go.
And sister wind let us down on the edge of this field,
Deep in the shade, beyond the perceptual acuities of the
 humans.
Here we sit to this day, in this moment,
Gazing out from behind yellow eyes,
Watching, waiting, thinking of nothing in particular.
Before there was language, there was nothing,
There were yellow gazing eyes...

Taeya

In this cool fall afternoon,
You who are you and I who am I,
Spoke briefly about the afternoon in our laboratory.
And the idiot instructor,
And the phantom lab partner who took so much of our
    time together,
Doing nothing...
And we laughed together about all of this,
And the red and yellow leaves were everywhere and
    everything,
When I fell in love with you so simply and most
    innocently.
In the glow of your charm and compassion,
And you had no time to go drink beer with me,
And I watched you walk to your car under the wet, silent
    trees,
You who are perfectly beautiful in the most physical and
    erotic way,
As I realized there is no more perfect moment than the
    smiles and the almost touching
Of two human beings standing in the cool fall afternoon
    of one single eternity on planet earth...

Two young boys on Halloween night
Went running down the backstreets of north Tacoma
With bags full of nothing and eyes full of candles and
    cats and witches
Everything was new on this black and orange night, and
    the girls knew it too
Donna and Debbie and a sister or two

Came fluttering along with the wind who coldly blew into the warm down jackets
And mittens we wore
I was in magic and apart from the world again like every dark evening when we all took Loose in the neighborhood
Our lives were so young and free and enchanted by the jack-o-lanterns and candles
The animals really did sense something special in the air, and I was moving into some new secret dimension
Our houses all looked sort of the same, but there was an emergent glow and energy from somewhere beyond normal, and all of a sudden, no adults existed.
Yes, I could hear things from down the street that were so far away, like a wolf...
I could see from above, like the birds, the crows and the eagle hawks...
It was the one time of year that the earth spoke to me, like another person, another soul
And I became limitless, without boundaries.
In I flowed, and out I flowed, and I could not explain it to anyone.
There was no time for that.
Would you listen to me?

Summer Solstice

Did you say that I was like the fog?
Did you find me shimmering along the coast one gray morning with the gulls?
Was I luminous, in shroud as the spirits of the elder parents who also dwell there?
Perhaps then you have seen me.
Perhaps you touched some subtle essence of my soul, as the remnants of me spread across the universe like the shedding spores of some giant bipedal mushroom.
It may be that you are in my footsteps.
I have walked this way before you.
This is no grand event, for I am nothing to you.
I am One Who Waits, and I am one who walks along the water's edge while others slumber.
I know you lie comfortably in your clean warm sheets, as my eyes travel the vast distances of space, in compressed, distorted time, along the invisible networks that join all things.
I am here frolicking in the wordless, noiseless void that rolls across the flat roaring ocean, so far I cannot imagine.
Until I am so far gone over blue oceans that my mind expands to my soul and it is only with effort that I return, to be in this physical body.
Here I seek your divine essence, for all who have lost their vision.
I saw you for the briefest of moments, standing alone as a dark speck flickering near the dune grasses in the southern skies.

The image of you was a non-constant wave of blue and
    gray light, and I know you thought desperately of
    calling across the huge sandy beach.
I beckoned for you to come, with the most subtle wave of
    my hand across my breast.
The sandpipers watched as they came crashing into the
    shallow streams of tide waters, seeking shrimps
    and clams for their next meal.
Just as suddenly I look down from the stars and there I
    lose you.
Just as I know you must, you are returning to the long
    hallways of your home in the city, and the tide is
    pressing me along.
You are blind to the wind that draws me.
As I am just now learning to see.
I will pass along to you those things that I find, as I can,
    in whatever way I can, believe me.
This is now the singular most important thing to me.
It is my human love for you.
I see one mother crying for her young daughter, barely a
    woman, and her body rotted with cancer.
I see how the Gods and deities of the ages of the earth
    are fallen and crumbling in the sands of time.
The large rubber heel of my boot strikes and crushes the
    empty shell of a sand dollar.
I draw my hands closer into the deep pockets of my
    overcoat, and shudder at the bite of the wind
    swirling over my skin.
I lie at the bottom of the blue ocean, look up at you and
    wonder.
Without my eyes, how will I see?
As I am unable to see, how will I know?

How will my sisters and brother, and how will all my children whom I love as well and just as great, and my parents who have gone before me in their gigantic strength and will, how will they consume me and be with me?

I notice the breach and crashing slap of the salmon moving invisibly in the water around me.

I casually allow my left hand to fall to my side, and reach stupidly for your hand, my fingers curling tightly around themselves in the numb, ice filled night...

Songs From Deep Regions

I, in merry shroud...
I passed a room of mist and drear,
An old woman gnarled a finger near,
Come tell me tales I long to hear,
Sweet words for wrinkled ears,
Smile as you recount the years.
Woman will you listen well,
To a song from lands where demons dwell?
Will you mind each note and tear,
I sing this song for you to hear.
Gray the dawn upon the day,
I took to walk this weary way,
No lamp in the doorway shone,
When to the streets I stepped alone.
Through the dimming town I wore,
With aching feet my burden bore,
A feeling never felt before,
I knew it, knowing nothing more.
Gone into the gloom I crept,
And there a sleepy maiden wept,
With ghostly lips I heard her smile,
Phantoms we, who slept a while.
I rose to the window beneath the moon,
From sheets of gray and silver noon,
Watching over the roadway scuttling geese and rats,
Who came to sit by where I sat,
Watching them waiting to speak when I spat on them,
Trampling their bodies and laughing uproariously.
Never the less,
Winter was the waxing moon,

A fragrant shift illuminating the stars,
Turning into pretty jars the seasons of a maidens room.
Fortune leaned on a post like a dark hour,
With misery a coin in his fingered pocket, unspent and
    wearisome,
For no more than the coarsest man, as much as kings...

Meeting Old Friends

From where I sit, I have not gone,
I do not sit, I linger on.
To where I wander here around,
Swiftly moving on the ground.
Coming when I walk along,
I settle down, the early dawn.

One Drop

Bound in lines trapping,
On the climbs wrapping,
All hands clapping together.
Sound voices weaving,
Wet clouds heaving,
Every cell cleaving one feather.

Mary

I suddenly rainbow love,
Waking to the new color you,
Undoing like some new rain,
The workings of time within me.
Bright water pearl blue, crazy who,
So mysteriously tender do,
Did we the honor of touching?
We wish, my only was you.
There lightly strolls a figure,
Wading into the night,
Who rolls a memory fading,
Through scattered speckles of light.

Night Watch

When darkness pervades and voids are abounding,
Then are my senses keen.
After midnight, when the hills ring,
Coal black the moon beams!
In low light, when winds sing,
Clear bright the night seems.
By doom shade my hope wings,
Wonders wide the earth brings!

Wands

I dreamed dark in deep night,
Borne full I watched a tempest grow,
Bright clouds broke and a storm blew,
Shrill and clear with ever-might,
It smote me hard and strong.
Walking low about lazy hills,
Lush and green lay shimmering vales,
Tossed in brandy winds like honey shale,
Lingering, I was alone,
The high sky was cold and still.
It shook my hair and eyes...
Stealthy breath I hold aloft, tears pour out my hands,
Heart worn lives leaning down, soft receding wands,
Footsteps pass away and drift, far, I go beyond.

Patty Jo

It is for you I come, my illustrious gypsy,
When the day is full and noon night,
Under the moon I watch for thee,
Waiting, waiting, patiently...
Here I sit, these months of years now,
Leaves in my hand, blown by occasional winds,
To scurry across your porch at early evening.
Follow intently their rustling trail,
Mark them, as if they were tears that fell,
Wet through your window, like footsteps through rain.
I must have been mad those days,
Do you remember?
That I never took you by the hand,
Or put a finger to quiet your breath in the night,
In the stillness to feel your heart.
You fear to touch the beams of the moon,
Magic stuff of dreams woven...I know you are
    somewhere listening.
There is a castle in a far cloud,
A white steed prancing with a golden mane,
One man standing tall and proud,
For his gypsy bride to come again...

Bright Eyes

O' bright eyes, have you heard?
Trumpets of the late season?
The march catastrophic?
Sirens off the coast?

In A Garden Bright

There is a garden full with seed,
Lain to rest like sage weed,
Sprouts spring like swamp reed,
I go there in dark deed and drink down the warm mead...
There walks a woman in the garden bright,
Her gaze fixed across the far night,
Over fields in earth light,
In her eyes the sparkle of star white,
I seek her gold by no man's right.

Song of November

Well, death rides a whirlwind over august moons,
While risen I running softly you down,
Come scattering orange leaves on the black pavement...

Water

There was a day when water was rainbows,
And only the sky knew why.

When I Die

When I die, die,
When I die, die, die,
I will die outside my body.

Mary in Rainbows

Walk with the winkling eye willow,
Dance the rainbow curtains wide.
Several crows in sleepy rows,
Would have you for their youngly bride.
Now I am told the wind is cold,
That many backs grow cracked and old,
And now I see how the years run long,
And gold fades in the pale dawn.
With hairy toes the crows in rows,
Watch a willow open, close,
Wait, bright eyes, for one surprise,
Suddenly spring on the rise.

Is The Unwrapping Done

Come, here, I have something for you.
Tell, I told,
Yes, you know what I hold.
Something hot, so oh very, not too quite cold?
I came sleepwalking waking into the old,
Newness, whoness, brought you in?
Well come, we are one,
Be at home, my you've grown.
Aren't that odd? Just nod,
Save the ribbons for next year?
No, O' I love you too much for that dear...

O' Stranger

O' Stranger please where might I find,
This lady so lovely of mine?
It was just yesterday, they took her away,
O' stranger please where might I find?
She is fragile my lady, my dame,
She is tender as no man has seen.
I miss her, you see, which is why I must flee,
Like a madman lost in the rain.
At night by my side she would stay,
And we laughed like children at play,
And they said she was wrong, when they took her along,
To a land where children are clay.
I look for her now, where the mountains bow,
Running alone to the sea.
For one so small, she isn't at all,
I weep like a child by the sea.
I'll never cease to pursue her release,
From that fortress cold and tall,
For she is breath, and although it means death,
I will bring down those iron walls.
O' stranger please where might they hide,
The little girl I've just described?
She's not lost at all, I still hear her call,
O' tell me please, where might they hide?

Letters To My Friend

Dearest sweetest Faith...

    If this heart could come somehow through the looking glass,
    And sit with you in the cool summer rain,
    Then would I take my only selves away and strip naked to the light and dark that are my essential being,
    To show you that I betray neither one nor the other,
    I am the eyeless beast of paradise, and make no other claim, ask no penance or forgiveness, as I am the impartial center of the stone. Chip all away, and you have all that is me, all that is nothing about the carbon tube that spins around this wild house of the universe, observing, enjoying.
    I have no malice for you, nor for any other.
    I must assume the veils of interpretation that cloud our vision periodically have somehow altered or confounded your vision of me, and what I am, and a simple thing that I have tried to do.
    My only, singular intent with this silly classmates tool was to alert as many people as I could that someone would help with the administrative organization of a reunion for the 40th out-year since we left that red brick institution on Orchard Street. My response to your posting was simply an attempt to clarify what appeared to be a duplicate, redundant event, and nothing else. I have no sense of ownership with this place, except to help any casual reader make sense from what others are planning. Perhaps we could jointly develop ideas, etc.

for this event, and act as co-chairs? This is what I had hoped for anyway, someone to share the development and broadcast the communication to others. My knowledge of prior reunion events is zero. I missed them all, for good or bad, for right or wrong, for no particular notion whatsoever. Land Sakes! my grandmother might say. *"I mean you no harm, Jenny Hayden"* - from *Starman, the movie.*

I have no idea why this happens. Why you offer up characterizations of who I am and what my motives or secondary and tertiary agendas might be. I try to speak clearly and directly with people for the most part. So, perhaps one day, if the Red Queen will allow, you and I might sit together and gently speak with understanding and compassion, and see each other again, as we did in the summers and spring times that carried us through high school. If my schedule and finances would allow, I would fly to your island tomorrow, and invite you away from the others, into some watery solitude, and then to show you who I am. Maybe I can explain the misunderstandings, maybe this is never possible. But I would try, at least, for we had something wonderful together, once upon a time in yesterday, and that was only just a moment from now...

This much I know. When two souls collide, stars everywhere will explode and redistribute their forces, and anything might happen...

Well, I am on schedule to finish my degree in June, and am in the "thesis" phase now. I am seeking employment, and looking for publishers for my book. When I have some extra cash, I will come to your island and invite you to my room, and you will come, or you will not. Call me sometime...gkj

My dearest darling

How then, can I get in to see your performance, or at the very least, your final rehearsal on Friday? What is the performance titled? How do I find you backstage, aside from wandering in like I own the place, as I often do. You would be surprised what people will take at face value, if you present your self from within, with no fear, with passion, and with resolve. Your writing style is equally as elegant as your physical beauty, and I am quickly becoming more deeply captured by your song, the song of you!

The song of the stories of all poets and lovers of time away, and time to come, as I humble my self to you, and seek only the soft touch of your mind and body in some hidden, secret way, to be discovered perhaps? Am I starting to sound a little bit like Frasier? OK, he is an adorable character, if way gone into some aberrant neuroses.

So, I wait patiently, and hope for the best. If you can bear my stillness, my love of sitting in the rose garden sipping wine, and holding hands, and talking just enough to notice the blue and white skies, and the smell of the darkening soils and forests, then become one with us, let us be two poets of some new kind, in this kaleidoscope world, beyond and merged with the summer of love, the year of Woodstock, and dreams of peace and love that our world keeps missing in the outside. Our gardens are well protected, and sanctuary from the madness, I can only hope. We will emerge together, as our arms wrap around our torsos, and out thighs entwine, and massage each other from below, and these two moist tongues slowly press into the deepness of our souls, and there is the only ecstasy beyond reason and nature, it is our physical joining, and the soft clean sheets of lavender. If you love me, as I know I love thee. gkj

[Are these poems mine? They are emergent, as you are my inspiration alone...as the bird remains on the branch, still, until the moment of flight presents its self]

Who Am I Today?

So today I look out the window
The rain and snow are mixed and falling in a loose
    pattern out on the street
The street over the bay of the ocean and my coffee is
    warm and sweet to my mouth
When I think of me and the clothes I wear
And what I am after all these years
And what I am not
This is my version of the Dr. Seuss for adults.
I am not the banker and I am not the lawyer
In their fine polished suits and starched underpants.
Then just now as I sit down again from my kitchen,
A huge thick flurry of snow blows down around the deck
    next to me
And the flakes are huge, they are growing now, and the
    spirit of the north wind is here
I see, my sister, from the top of this world.
I see. You are bringing to me the brother dingo
    Bodidharmas,
The friend I lost and who lives still in the magical
    kingdom around me.
This is not Walt Disney. But I love him anyway, for his
    concept,
His commitment to Imagineering
Yes, Walt, I know.
The snow continues to come down. I do believe.
This is the north god, assuring us the ice is here.
I am from the inside and out the Zen monk.
I shed the fancy clothes and fortunes.
The more I think the less I am.

The less I want. My house is now down to one small
   bedroom.
If I left today the furniture would go, and a few clothes
   would come along.
I think again of the shoulder pack, a small fuel stove,
   and some matches.
A nice over coat and some good boots that fit.
Or a good boat that fits. Nice also.
I am the oyster on the beach, ensconced in its shell, and
   filtering the water I bathe in.
If I never move, or become unsettled, the world will
   surround me.
So I got me some Buddha clothes, some nice loose baggy
   pajamas with
An Asian collar, and walk with loosely attached wrists,
   like a California fairy.
I like that. This is me. I am none of the other costumes I
   see around me.

North to Alaska, or the Story of Balto:

Do I cross this stretch of frozen ice to get my serum to Nome? Do I save an entire days travel over much worse, but perhaps safer routes that are over solid ground? The break up of the sea ice is already late this year...any day now. I ask the old Inuit hunter who stands behind me, and he nods his head slowly. We both look at the sky, and out across the frozen inlet. "You go first" he seems to say. I check my sled and my guns, and head forth with a lead dog who can smell 20,000 times better than me. He can smell the ice breaking, the spirits of his ancestors are all around you. Monitor and adjust, while the dogs run on and on...

Evgeniya, Ethereal Soviet

What is this miracle that you come across the ether within hours of me swiping my credit card on a whim to join this network of souls pursuing souls? And that you possess an inner soul fire on a depth with my own, and that you see the fools on parade, and the sheep who are lost in the harbor, and the greed and stupidity of the masses? And that we are for each is obvious, and that there is only one thing to know, that when you return from your sojourn in Africa that you make your final aerial port destination "Seattle" and that I will greet you and will burst into my arms and plunge your tongue to the depths of our entwining souls, and mine own eyes shall melt into yours and we will no longer sense our two selves as individuals any longer, as I am devoted to you and you only, as you are to me? This I know, this can be the only explanation for this pure miracle that fluttered from the sky to land like a hummingbird in the I that was me only just an eternity before, and am forever changed in these early moments of your experience and presence...and now I am still, for the words seem trivial, as some distant energetic spirit completes me, and it is you, I, we, and the morning sky was never so clear and sweet, as it is this new morning in this wholly new universe.

[Are these poems mine? They are emergent, as you are my inspiration alone...as the bird remains on the branch, still, until the moment of flight presents its self]

All my stars for thee...gkj

Note to ....

I have not even met you, yet I seem to be missing you, just knowing you are not available to write to or talk to, even though I know you will be home soon. I picture you sitting in your little cabin on the pond, cross legged in bed with the fire glowing and the candles flickering, and a book or computer in your lap, slowly rocking and smiling at nothing in particular, perhaps the night air scenting your sheets like some earthly divine perfume? And then I am beside you, with my hand resting lightly on your inner thigh, since it is so easily accessible just under the soft cottony shirt you wear that comes down just to above your knees, and when you sit, it slightly rides up exposing your smooth, cool skin just up to below your hips and the full round flesh of your bottom. It seems so simple and natural that as I feel you next to me, and the soft damp breath of you moves into the room, and I smell the body that is you inside and out, and breathe you into me as well. Slipping slowly, I trace the curve of your leg with my right hand softly up into the round smooth skin that indicates your feminine urgencies, so moist and throbbing gently in the fleshiness of your parted thighs, still cross legged, and flexing a little as I move my long finger inside you, parting the flesh and sliding into the long tight opening that leads into your body. My flesh begins to swell between my own legs, and I seem to hurried as I turn and move onto you, rotating you to fall gently onto your back, and I take your legs apart, and move my mouth over you, slowly sucking and nuzzling the rapid breathing from deep inside you, as you quickly gasp, grabbing my head and pulling me into you, as you buck and spread your hips. So soon I am across and behind you, with one arm across your back pulling at your nipples, and you lift your leg up sideways so that we are both on our side, and my fully engorged male thing slips into your womanhood, pressing in and out, much too quickly but so intense that your screams begin as you come on me ,and the wet fluids gush over us and the hot slippery pumping fluid I give you mixes and pours out onto the sheets, as we throb and subside, and the reflex of you pumping my large thick rubbery meat just oozes me out and drains me, so natural , and so wonderful, and my hands are all over you, gently caressing and milking your flesh, as we give, as we take, and I arch my back one last time, empty, and full, and all this hot slick stuff is in you, on us, in the sheets...hmmm. Ok, so we will need lots of clean towels....

Hurry home!

6/12/08

Note to ....

I am totally enthralled with you, and will never engage your time for endless, constant meaningless blather on the phone. This I know you know, and only that I love you and all that is us and about me, about you, wrapped like a pita sandwich so we cannot escape our combined meats and savory bodily spices, juices, and this thick tongue of mine comes sneaking slowly up behind you into the sweet clean cleft of your bottom and pushes ever so slowly but with persistent strength deep into your tight pink hole, and you tingle up into your mind, as I push in and out, and the stars come open to your soul. This wet sweetness encircles your bottom, and pulls slowly out, then back in , and you push your hips back to me while I tongue fuck your butt. You love this, I feel the groans move through me....we play each other , and I am deeper into you than you ever thought possible...it is good for your hips. as you splay your self to allow me hot thing to move ever deeper into you, into you...and would you do the same for me, for your master, for your obedient slave, and pull your fingernails across my flesh at the same time, until the slightest red and pink trickles open up, while your fingers move deeper into my skin? Who is that at the window??

6/13/08

Note to my dream lover...

With my hand resting lightly in your lap, and you beside me nestled into our pillows, and the nice down coverlet cast over our legs and feet, with the fire crackling and the candles glowing as we gaze silently out into the starry starry night, and the river flows, and I feel you breathing, and your hand floats in my hand, and I am in perfect bliss, this coming of the high soaring of my life, into those clouds with thee as we go smiling, as giants strolling the universe in one long stride...and our bodies dissolve..

7/14/08

Note for Suzan

I carry your heart, I carry it in my heart,
And like a precious, rare bird who flutters inside me,
You remain safe and protected, for there is one integral fortress surrounding you, Architecturally sound with love and passion,
Knowing that what touches you, touches the foundation of my own power,
And so proceed, with this mutual knowledge into the rainbow sunrises of all tomorrows, Beyond time as we know it.

6/18/08

Note for mine...

I was wondering the same. But I was not alarmed, it seemed all right that someone would enjoy us being together and watching as we slipped over and around each others bodies. And to think she might also be touching her self as she enjoyed our pleasures, wishing she might quietly at some point slip into the moon darkened room and noiselessly come under the sheets with us, pressing her cupped hand between your legs and wiggling her finger up and into you, while you hover together over my belly, and I roll my fingers into your bottoms, and one or the other set of suckling lips tug and pull and suck on my nipples, little hard rubber things between the rolling of your tongues.

6/18/08

You who have become now the focus of my dreams and diurnal pleasures. Walk with me in the open nakedness of summer, and let our bodies swing and move through the refreshing air as it cools and bathes our secret and opened parts. Sit naked next to me on our wooden loungers, with soft cushions around us, and under you so we might turn and free our hands to explore your chest and belly and press my knee into your thighs, feeling the loosed full flesh of my groin against your smooth white skin...This is the single moment, beyond which there is no time. Nothing went before, and nothing follows. All time presents to consciousness as one moment. As I sit typing these words for us, nothing was, all that is presents in my consciousness. All that was passed or past, is now present, and only present as I conceive it. Close in behind me, and press your hips into mine, and reach around my waist with your strong slender hands and pull my bottom back into you, while your fingers scratch at the flesh between my legs, reaching way around pulling up the front, leaving red tracer lines all up my fleshy genitals and across my belly, as I bend down and feel you pressing into me deeper with your groin and the hard bone of your pelvis...you split me, and in a moment I become the feminine, overtaken by the fierce penetrating lust of you...do not stop, my loving one, go deeper, I am prepared for you deep down in my soul, into the flesh of me, and my now erect protuberance is pumped quickly and vigorously by your right hand, and then I erupt in a slick, slippery hot fluid that runs over your hands, lubricating my member, and we fall, and you pump deep inside me, I flex my muscle, and pull you deeper, into the dark vacuum of my insides, you swell and engorge, moving more slowly, as you empty into mine as well...thank you, for being this, for being all lovers in all ways for this smooth round flesh that lies now under you, squirming slightly with pleasure, and breathing deeply with the subsiding orgiastic mist...

Cantina Mia

In this small restaurant called La Fondita was the
    beautiful black haired angel,
She captured my voice the first time I saw her,
And I was never expecting it.
This little place and the cool darkness of the bar,
The smell of fruit juice, and the salt and the limes.
Her eyes were a deep penetrating vision that sunk
    deeply into my belly and heart,
Not the coy faint shallow smile that many pretty girls
    learn when they are young.
She was shaking my soul and it was the light of her soul,
That came into every cell of my being,
As if she was beckoning to me, to come find her, to
    become one with her.
For that one last event when the woman of dreams
    would emerge, find me,
And the rest would come about so simply,
Like the turn of a key in the never ending cosmos,
Our fingers engage, and we float in understanding.
Somewhere I heard the giant sasquatch named EJ was
    her fiancé.
How could this be so?
He is 8 feet tall and hairy, makes deep noises like the
    beast,
Do not go with him Senorita, he makes the world dark,
Your face becomes one hundred years past when he
    comes close to your body.
He would unwittingly and clumsily destroy what is
    pristine,
Generously stunning about your soul.

He is not of your way, not for your time,
Send him away, and let me love you until we die.
Take these tiny flowers I bought at the flower merchants
 today,
Keep them cool and wet, keep them in your sweet
 fragrance in your room,
Let their light show you my love, and the broader love
 that I bring for you.
These colors will paint your mind with the heart of me,
And this meaningless life, this self, that is me will go
 forward with you,
Engaging in soft caresses, cool skin on skin.
You may take my head in your slender fingers and guide
 my mouth to yours,
In this instant we will dance electric tongues and
 slippery cheeks around and around,
And your full warm breast is pressing into mine, and we
 are breathing quietly,

While the stars move slowly above, and one falling star
 splashes softly into the cool liquid pool that is
 your eyes...
Stepping one foot together into the rolling universe out
 there.
When stars collide, this must be the way they feel,
Every atom that is me becomes every atom that is you,
And we are never more in this world of known things...

And then it came,
That which is my terror in this loving universe,
That you are engaged...bound by the material world.
And you are bound to this world in your conceptual
 model of your self,
And now I feel I am thrust in some new galactic
 rendezvous,

And this was only the circle touching me again,
As we go around and around...
All the better for me,
In 10 years you will be fat, your tits will sag,
And the brats you spawn will suck the life out of you...

Song for All Seasons

These are the songs of the poets of all time,
Of all the days and nights that ever turned blue in the sunset hours,
We are here to paint the images of the dream time,
The world that is hidden to the rest of you,
And let you in through the other doorways,
Where your thoughts and minds seldom wander.

I stroll the fringes of your neighborhood,
And you may or may not see who I am, who we are,
But we know you.

We know what is your passion, your sense of loss, and why you rise each day,
Why you go on for more, and what is the mundane aspect of you.
With less apparent, we show you what is more,
We present what was in shadow in lighted form,
And hope that you will find us.

I come forth in the shadow lands, and may easily be missed.
If you hurry, or set your mind on trivia, then surely I will miss you,
I am only your earthen tablet if you take some measure of your self,
Do you find in the tiniest flower some hieroglyph?
Is there a message waiting here for you?
Were you contrived to become this thing you are today?
Or was there another path you missed somehow?

Here lies the garden of Alice, the Looking Glass and the rabbit's hole,
These subtle and obvious clues are all around you,
Reach out and touch them, they mean no harm but to enlighten,
Often to surpass your circle of knowledge,
And bring you to an alteration, a subtly retrieved metabolic state.
It was there all along, and you only miss it due to coincidence.

These road signs the poets leave will always be there.
So there is nothing to fear.
As nation states and the ruling classes often murder and suppress my kind,
We always reemerge as the fungus beneath your feet emerge,
Following a cool autumn rain.
Go ahead, stop, reach down and touch my body,
It will do you no harm, and may bring you entire worlds of something beneficial,

Please sit upon this bench, this fallen giant of the forest,
Whose roots form a perfect cradle for your human body,
And then settle back, looking up at the blue sky and the whiter clouds,
And allow these images to float toward you, until they enter your mind,
Flow through your eyes, and you forget all the words of history,
All the science, and other dogma of the eons.
Come find me there, as you will know me easily,
I am floating there now, somewhere over China,
And will come to visit you in this moment.
Do you feel it? Is the subtle glow of me filling your body?

The End

www.ingramcontent.com/pod-product-compliance
Lightning Source LLC
Chambersburg PA
CBHW031630160426
43196CB00006B/352